This book is dedicated to

Every parent of a gifted child
Every woman who has struggled between family and a career
Everyone interested in science—and to everyone with any interest
in the stars, galaxies, and space.

My Daughter Beatrice

*A Personal Memoir
of Dr. Beatrice Tinsley, Astronomer*

Edward Hill

Published by The American Physical Society
New York

Copyright © 1986 by The American Physical Society

ISBN 0-88318-493-1

Library of Congress Cataloging-in-Publication Data

Hill, Edward.
    My daughter Beatrice.

    1. Tinsley, Beatrice M. 2. Astronomers—New
Zealand—Biography. I. Title.
QB36.T56H55 1986   520'.92'4 [B]   86—13974

Published by The American Physical Society
through the American Institute of Physics

Printed in the United States of America

The American Physical Society
335 East 45th Street
New York, NY 10017-3483

CONTENTS

FOREWORD

When Dr. Sandra Faber of the Lick Observatory in California told me that the American Astronomical Society was instituting a medal and prize in honour of my daughter Beatrice, I realised that she would be widely remembered as a scientist. At the same time I thought that there are people who would like to know more about her as a person.

Her memorial service at Yale was described as a "celebration of a beautiful life," and who knew more about that beautiful life than myself? For I have not only memories going right back to the day of her birth, but treasures of her childhood kept by her mother, many of her school reports and, above all, hundreds of her letters. These extend over twenty-three years, from her first week as a university student at Canterbury to her last days as a professor at Yale.

So, thinking especially of Beatrice's family and friends in New Zealand, Britain, and the Americas, I offer this personal tribute to a wonderful daughter.

EDWARD O. E. HILL

INTRODUCTION

This is a remarkable book, about an unusual person under unusual circumstances. Beatrice Muriel Hill Tinsley was a wife, mother, teacher, and above all, a passionate and gifted astrophysicist. Fatally afflicted in mid-career by melanoma, she had by that time already produced a body of research worthy of a full lifetime's effort.

The present volume tells Beatrice's story from three points of view. The first and fullest is a loving portrait written by her father, Edward Hill. This in itself is noteworthy. It is rare when a famous scientist is survived by a parent, and rarer still when that parent is motivated and able to write with such insight, clarity, and memory for detail. Mr. Hill's description of Beatrice in primary school, with teddy bears, violin, and self-imposed schedules, is enchanting to those of us who knew her as an adult. We can trace the early intensity and joyous enthusiasm for life that were later so striking in the grown woman.

A second viewpoint, briefer and more formal, is to be found in the obituary written by two friends and colleagues, Prof. Richard Larson and Dr. Linda Stryker. Their account is a faithful and factual summary of the high points of Beatrice's life and the significance of her research work as seen by peers in the field. In daily contact with Beatrice at Yale, they provide a vivid description of her place in the Yale Astronomy Department and the extraordinary, galvanizing effect she had on that institution.

This Introduction offers yet a third perspective, that of good friend and professional colleague, but someone who was located across the country, and who, save for a short six-month period, saw Beatrice only briefly at scientific meetings or symposia. We two interacted mostly by letter and telephone. Despite the distance, Beatrice exerted a powerful influence on me, the way I thought about astronomy, and my developing set of scientific standards. My reminiscences provide yet another valid portrait of Beatrice, for she kept up similar friendships with many other astronomers. As a result her influence extended far beyond the halls of Yale and was felt, literally, wherever galaxy evolution was an active subject.

Edward Hill's memoir is generous in personal anecdotes but understandably brief in its discussion of astronomical science. Larson and Stryker's account is fuller on this subject but was written for an audience knowledgeable about astronomy and cosmology. In this Introduction, it seems appropriate to place Beatrice's research work in perspective for readers unacquainted with astronomy. In so doing, one comes to appreciate better why her life history holds so much fascination and what lessons it offers for creative young people, themselves just embarking on adulthood.

One might say that I first met Beatrice Tinsley by reading her Ph.D. thesis. I was struggling with my own thesis at the time and was consciously seeking a good model to emulate. I read the thesis diligently every night between 1 and 2 A.M. before bed, and in a week I had finished it, deeply impressed. Beatrice's distinctive scientific style was already remarkably well developed in this, her first major publication. The arguments were lucid, the presentation meticulous, the writing itself graceful yet economical—the net impact could best be described as "lean."

Scientifically it was also an outstanding achievement. Suffice it to say that Beatrice had had to learn a great many disciplines—stellar evolution, stellar atmospheres, the interstellar medium, galaxies, computer programming—and pull them all together to formulate her conclusions. This was at a time, 1967, when these disciplines were still rather separate from one another, without much shared knowledge between fields. I was greatly impressed that anyone, let alone a student, could write so authoritatively in so many different areas. In so doing, the author of this thesis had clearly set a new and higher standard for research on galaxies and had shown the way to a much greater degree of realism in models of galaxy evolution. It was also uncomfortably clear that the rest of the world, including myself, would have to run very hard to keep up.

To understand why Beatrice's thesis was so successful and why her career as a whole had such an impact on astronomy, it is necessary to digress for a moment about the nature of astronomy generally and her specialty, galaxies, in particular. Astronomy is an extraordinarily cohesive and synthetic discipline. It differs from the laboratory sciences in that the events under study are far removed both in space and also in time. Astronomers thus resemble detectives, who come upon the scene of a crime after all the interesting events have happened. Worse, they cannot actually visit the scene itself but must content themselves with making sketchy observations from afar—how rapidly a certain star is moving, whether a galaxy rotates or not, and so on. Like detectives, astronomers often make progress by collecting subtle and seemingly unrelated clues—clues that, once assembled, can reveal new and unexpected astronomical truths.

Because of its synthetic nature, astronomy might aptly be termed the crossroads of physics. For the same reason, galaxy evolution certainly must be considered the crossroads of astronomy. Galaxies are among the most fascinating objects in the Universe. Each one is highly complex, containing a 100 billion or so stars, thousands of star clusters, gigantic clouds of interstellar gas, tangled magnetic fields, swarms of cosmic rays—the whole in grand, stately rotation orchestrated by the force of gravity. New generations of stars continuously coalesce within dense clumps of interstellar gas, in so-called "stellar nurseries." Each star eventually exhausts its thermonuclear fuel supply of light elements and dies, shriveling to a cold, dead relic. In dying, some stars explode violently, disgorging their hot, radioactive ashes back into the interstellar medium. This cycle of birth, death, and replenishment is repeated millions of times, but the trend is inevitably downward. Each star uses more gas than it returns, and thus a galaxy, like a fire, must gradually consume all its fuel and go out. Galactic death is not yet apparent to us, the whole process taking perhaps 100 billion years, far longer than the present 10–20 billion year age of the Universe. However, it looms on the distant horizon.

Galaxies are not only complex internally, they also congregate in an interesting array of structures larger than themselves. After galaxies coalesced initially out of the Big Bang, pairs of galaxies began to fall together, then groups, then clusters and still larger, "superclusters"—all by mutual gravitational attraction. The result—huge swarms of galaxies and vast, empty voids between—constitutes the landscape of today's universe. To survey it, we count galaxies and map their distribution in space, out to the limits of the largest telescopes. Galaxies are indeed the basic building blocks of the Universe and the raw material of cosmology.

Ranging from the tiniest stars to the horizons of the Universe, the field of galactic research incorporates essentially all astronomical knowledge. A special quality of mind is required to encompass a subject at once so detailed and so vast, and this is where Beatrice Tinsley excelled. When she began her work, the life-cycle story of galaxies sketched above was only dimly apparent. Beatrice was thus inspired to commence a systematic program to explore essentially every aspect of galaxy evolution. Initially alone and later with many collaborators, she calculated accurately how stellar populations age, how they change in luminosity and color, and at what rate and in what proportions they convert pure hydrogen and helium into heavier elements via nuclear burning. She estimated the age of the Universe from isotope ratios of uranium and thorium, traced the production of heavy elements in the halo and disk of the Galaxy, and tested systematically whether every known phase of stellar evolution would have observable consequences in the light of galactic stellar populations. A favorite subject, for example, was stellar death, on which she wrote several times. In one paper charmingly entitled "Necrology of the Hyades Cluster," she used the known age of the Hyades star cluster to deduce an upper limit to the mass of stars that die peacefully as white dwarfs. Another paper explored the progenitor masses of certain kinds of supernovae explosions by analyzing statistically where in galaxies they occur: in spiral arms populated by young, massive stars, or between arms, where stars are smaller and older.

The knowledge thus gained was constantly applied to improve models of galaxy evolution. Over the years, Beatrice and collaborators were increasingly able to keep track of the complicated internal workings of a typical galaxy. A major addition, with Larson's help, was the inclusion of motions induced by gravity during the initial collapse phase. What resulted from the total program were the first plausible pictures of what protogalaxies might have looked like when forming billions of years ago.

Not only did Beatrice pioneer in the internal physics of galaxies, she also led in exploring interactions between galaxies and their environment, processes that are now widely acknowledged to affect their evolution profoundly. She provided strong impetus to the study of galaxy collisions and mergers, which she and Larson argued can cause a sudden burst of new stars. Another fascinating idea was "stripping," a process whereby the interstellar gas within some galaxies is swept out as the galaxies orbit through the diffuse gas that permeates large clusters. Loss of "fuel" by this process can clearly hasten a galaxy's death and send it to an early grave. Yet another interesting phenomenon explored by Beatrice was "dynamical friction," in which heavy cluster galaxies lose energy and spiral down to the cluster center, there to collect in a gigantic "supergalaxy." Such monsters are actually observed and outweigh our own Milky Way by perhaps a hundred times. On these subjects and others, Beatrice wrote key papers that helped to transform radical ideas into respected, fundamental concepts that underlie galaxy research today.

As noted, a major contribution that Beatrice brought to her program of galaxy research was the greatly heightened degree of accuracy and realism in model galaxy calculations. This was due in part to the fact that her models relied on detailed computer programs rather than the simplified, analytic formulas that had previously been used. A second key ingredient was her intimate familiarity with the myriad astronomical processes that properly belonged in the models, including stellar evolution, dynamics, and nuclear physics. In this, she showed a degree of mastery that no one else, before or since, has attained. With her death, the construction of accurate galaxy evolution models that combine detailed treatment of stellar evolution with spatial motions and dynamical behavior has, at least for the present, effectively ceased.

A principal byproduct of the evolution program was the concept of galaxies as changing, evolving entities whose properties can change discernibly over timescales fairly short compared to the age of the Universe. This idea, one of Beatrice's most significant contributions, has inspired a whole new school of galactic studies that uses the so-called "lookback" effect to observe galaxies as they were at earlier times. Astronomers are able to do this by making use of the only true time machines at human disposal—large telescopes. Astronomical distances are so vast that it takes light a finite time to reach us: eight minutes from the Sun, four years from the nearest star, two million years from the nearby Andromeda galaxy. Viewing the Virgo cluster of galaxies, we see events there as they were 50 million years ago, when the last dinosaurs walked here on Earth. This is still quite close by cosmic standards. With the largest optical telescopes at our disposal and very long exposure times, the night sky is seen to be literally blanketed with tiny, faint smudges of light, so numerous that their images begin to overlap. These are distant galaxies at the edge of the observable universe, and, by the best reckoning, the light of many of them has taken well over 10 billion years to reach us. Their age as viewed by us is therefore just a few billion years old, veritable youngsters compared to the 10- to 20-billion-year-old galaxies closer to home.

It is now a grand dream of modern cosmology to elucidate galactic evolution by zeroing in on the differences between these youngsters and the older galaxies nearby. A major problem, though, is to discern the structure of the distant ones clearly enough. Their images are tiny, and the vital details of their spiral structure, rotating disks, interactions, mergers, and so on are smeared out and erased by the blurring effects of the Earth's atmosphere. The Hubble Space Telescope, a new large observatory to be placed in space above the atmosphere, is expected to change all this. Free of atmospheric blurring, HST's sharper images will shrink the apparent viewing distance to faraway galaxies by a factor of 10 to 20. Astronomers the world over are now planning major programs to study distant galaxies with HST, presently scheduled for launch in 1987. These and related ground-based studies constitute a major thrust of modern cosmological research. The current surge of interest in distant galaxies can be traced directly to the intellectual legacy of Beatrice Tinsley.

Though the memory of her scientific contributions lives on, impressions of Beatrice as a person remain equally vivid in the minds of friends. Of these, the most remarkable to me was her all-consuming energy and passion for astronomy. This was usually a great stimulus for colleagues, but could at times be rather intimidating. Many times Beatrice would turn up bright and early in the morning, trailing graphs and computer output that fully answered the questions you and she had barely managed to formulate the afternoon before. On one occasion at a scientific meeting, Beatrice presented me at breakfast with a draft of a paper she had finished the previous night. She requested my comments, and, since she was invariably the most careful reader of my own papers, I wanted strongly to return the favor. I therefore stayed up late that night reading the rather complicated and lengthy analysis. Coming down the next morning, I was armed with cogent observations and ready for a good discussion. To my surprise, however, Beatrice presented me with yet another paper on a totally different subject but, like its predecessor, completed just the night before. My cherished chance to interact with scientific colleagues at the meeting was fast evaporating, what with reading Beatrice's papers! The forebodings of earlier years were indeed coming true—it was proving hard work to keep up.

Along with the passion and concentration, however, went an uncommon generosity and interest not only in the research work but also in the personal well-being of others. Beatrice paid attention and was a receptive listener. As noted, she was the best critic of my own papers, and she did the same favor for many others. In consequence, she became a clearinghouse for new results, playing the vital role of coordinator and communicator in a field where many different inputs had to be evaluated and synthesized. Beatrice won the reputation as the "Whole Earth Catalog" of galactic studies. She knew who was doing what and could put you in contact with just the person you needed to talk to. No one before or since has played this role to such perfection, and the communications gap left by her passing is as much missed, I believe, as the cessation of her scientific output.

Beatrice's outer-directedness and concern for others was especially apparent during her long struggle with cancer. When it began, I myself was laid up in bed with a back problem that lasted several weeks and was much depressed with my slow rate of recovery. Beatrice somehow heard and telephoned to cheer me up, mentioning casually at the time that she, too, was in the hospital—undergoing surgery for melanoma. My heart stopped; I knew how virulent the disease could be. The very next day, a further surprise arrived—a beautiful plant from Beatrice to brighten my room. This display of concern from someone whose own health was in an infinitely more precarious state was most touching, but typical of her.

Much later, when the cancer was clearly gaining ground, Beatrice entered the Yale Infirmary for what was to be her final stay. I flew over twice from California, and the visits are etched deeply in my mind. After an initial struggle, Beatrice's calm acceptance of terminal illness was extraordinarily frank and open. Her attitude made it possible to discuss the most dreadful possibilities with no greater unease, it seemed, than the morning news. Feeling comfortable, friends came to visit in large numbers, and they kept the place lively. No subject was sacred, including the comical, awful wig she adopted when radiation treatments caused the loss of her hair. In the elevator on one of those occasions, I inquired of a nurse from Beatrice's floor what it was like to have a terminally ill cancer patient in what was basically a student infirmary. "Well," she confided, "we were a little worried in the beginning about the depressing effects on the students, of course. But it's not been like that at all. Professor Tinsley and her friends are cheering us all up!"

In conclusion, I would like to return to a question raised earlier and explore what lessons Beatrice's life history holds for scientists, indeed, creative people everywhere. A key point, it seems to me, is that Beatrice set a high moral tone. Her friendliness, open-mindedness, encouragement of younger people, and, especially, her scientific honesty all contributed greatly to her reputation. Scientists in every discipline can find in Beatrice's career a model for how the scientific enterprise at its best should operate. Nonscientists can draw the more general conclusion that upright, caring, ethical behavior enhances an individual's influence rather than the reverse. This is a lesson worth heeding in today's competitive world.

A second point is more sensitive. No account of Beatrice's life would be complete without mention of what for her was a major and continuing problem: how to balance commitments to family and career. The many difficulties that she met early in life—the controversy and resistance that her views of galaxy evolution aroused in some quarters, the hard time she had in finding a permanent appointment—these and other problems were eventually solved, and Beatrice, I believe, was satisfied at the outcome. The problem with her family was never fully solved, however, especially the difficult decision to leave her children at home and take up work elsewhere. Beatrice felt long-term sorrow, remorse, and guilt over this step, feelings that were never fully expiated.

The special unhappiness that Beatrice bore in the wake of this decision must be ascribed in considerable part to the fact that she was a woman. In our society, husbands commonly divorce their spouses and leave children behind, and many seem to do so with a fairly clear conscience; it is an accepted thing. A woman's duty to her children, however, is held to be more binding. Women like Beatrice with children and careers are thus under a special, double burden. To conclude that Beatrice escaped this burden by living separately would be quite wrong— she bore it, but in a different way.

Why Beatrice felt driven to make such a choice is described elsewhere in this volume. Here I simply offer two observations. The first is the truism that, in any career, there is a huge infusion of luck. Sudden job opportunities, pregnancies, illness, the evolving needs of oneself and one's spouse, all these arise unexpectedly and can deflect the best-laid plans. Like everyone else, Beatrice and her family fell victims to such accidents, which created hard choices with no easy answers.

Fortunately, a second, more constructive observation also emerges. Much of Beatrice's trouble can be traced, I believe, to a failure early enough to realize what an unusual person she truly was. She knew she was keen on astrophysics but did not comprehend how central a role it had to play in her life. This ignorance of her true nature led her to take on personal commitments that later proved to be insupportable. Many individuals in her childhood were impressed with her talents and many encouraged her, but not many, it seems, took her aside and urged her to look deeply within herself, to question whether the conventional path of marriage and children was the best way for her, a budding scientist, to enter adult life. To the contrary, it appears that there was overwhelming pressure to push her in traditional directions.

In conclusion, then, I would argue that the following pages should be read as an account of one individual's voyage of self-discovery and awakening. As such, it may stimulate each one of us to reexamine critically the goals and aspirations we have for our own lives. Even more, it may inspire us to take a more active interest in helping those around us do likewise, especially the young people among us. To aspire consciously to the role of mentor, advisor, or just friendly listener would be a fitting tribute indeed to Beatrice; these are roles for which she herself is now most fondly remembered.

SANDRA M. FABER, Lick Observatory

March 1986

CHAPTER ONE

War Baby

1941–1945

Beatrice was born prematurely at Richmond Lodge, Chester, in northwest England on January 27th, 1941. Snow lay on the ground and cold fog filled the air. Late in the afternoon I was called home from Western Command headquarters, where I was a staff captain, and was greeted by a nurse telling me not to expect a live baby. Some hours later, however, I heard a small cry coming from the bathroom, connected by a sliding door to the bedroom where my wife Jean was lying. The doctor had worked hard to make the little scrap of humanity draw her first breath.

There was no question of an incubator or sterilised baby ward. Bathroom and bedroom were warmed by a portable oil heater and a coal fire. The baby was put in a cot beside her mother and the doctor left ordering us to keep the room at seventy degrees Fahrenheit.

The previous weeks had been punctuated by air raids. Chester was not a prime target, but near enough to Liverpool to receive bombs from planes which could not or would not penetrate the anti-aircraft defences of the important docks. A few weeks earlier our attic's ceiling had bulged ominously and the back door had lost its latch, when a bomb exploded in the railway yards over the fence behind the house. We had heard it coming and thrown ourselves on the floor. In fact we had heard two 'whistles' and only one explosion, so spent an apprehensive

1

night. The disposal squad removed the unexploded bomb next day.

These conditions may well have contributed to the baby being so premature, but as it turned out she chose her time of arrival well, for the wintry conditions continued and for over a month there were no air raids. Our chief problem was to keep the room warm enough. Coal was rationed and, with snow all around, no deliveries had been possible for some time. Richmond Lodge, for all its grandiose name, was fortunately no more than an enlarged cottage with small rooms and low ceilings. But heating even the bedroom would have been impossible had it not been that we then had a most devoted elderly married couple, who had followed us from our pre-war home at Llandaff on the edge of Cardiff. The man, George, called on all our unknown neighbours with a coal scuttle, told the story of our emergency and found a ready response. So the fire was kept going and wee Beatrice thrived till she reached her proper birth date. Then the thaw came and with it more air raids, which would have been terrifying if mother and baby had still been confined to an upstairs room.

I recall very well the day of Beatrice's christening. Her two grandmothers had come from their homes out in the countrysides of Cumberland and Monmouthshire and, after spending the previous evening at Richmond Lodge, had walked back to their hotel in the centre of Chester. Soon afterwards an ear-shattering explosion broke every pane of glass over a wide area, but by great good fortune the bomb, which would have destroyed almost all of the famous old Chester 'rows,' had gone off in mid-air. The grandmothers, so far from feeling nervous, were glad to have shared something of what much of the nation was enduring! But in the morning we learned that Liverpool had suffered most terribly and that afternoon, as we were finishing the party which followed the actual christening, a young man I had known slightly before the war as a rather feckless bachelor appeared at the door in merchant navy uniform accompanied by his recently married wife. She was deadly pale and had grime on her face, having clearly been through an ordeal. Staying in a hotel by the Liverpool docks she had watched and heard an ammunition ship blow up in the harbour, close to where her husband, whom she had come to bid farewell on his next voyage, was fighting fires on his ship. Neither of them had had anything to eat since the previous day, so it was providential that we had managed to obtain enough extra food for our party to be able to feed them at a time when rationing made giving extra meals extremely difficult! He was taking her to friends in the country before joining his ship, and I hope the sight of a family rejoicing over a new life did something to restore her shattered morale.

Soon afterwards my mother asked Jean to take the children to her home in the country for the summer. Our elder daughter, Rowena, was singularly unaffected by air raids. She had even slept through the explosion which so nearly shattered the house. But Jean was not picking up well after Beatrice's birth, and the maternity nurse, who had stayed on to care for the tiny baby, was pleased with the idea that she would have total peace in the country. I was left with George and his good wife Cissie, while Beatrice was also well cared for. My old Nannie still held a somewhat undefined but vital role in my mother's household and, when the time came that Jean found a permanent nannie for our two children, there were a couple of days when no less than three nannies were concerned with the newest arrival! Jean found this very funny, especially as she was writing to me while lying in a chaise longue under a cedar tree, looking out over a wide stretch of beautiful country and reading a book entitled "The Single-handed Mother"! I mention all this because Nannie Gullidge, who then joined our family, became a very important part of Beatrice's life for many years. An experienced children's nurse, she had recently married in her late forties and been tragically widowed within a few months. She came to us trying to pick up the threads of her life again, and with pent-up love to bestow on her new charge. It was returned in full measure! With great common sense she immediately stripped off the extra covers with which the aging maternity nurse had been coddling her baby, and, with summer sun in my mother's beautiful garden, small Beatrice flourished. Some time in the autumn the family returned to Chester, and Jean's photograph album contains snapshots taken the following spring showing a robust one-year-old with exceptionally bright eyes.

Shortly after that we moved house again. Richmond Lodge was close to the river Dee and, while dry in itself, was surrounded by an atmosphere that was very often damp. Rowena developed rheumatism and there was fear of rheumatic fever, which had been an affliction in Jean's family. So the doctor pronounced that we must get away from the river.

3

At the time Chester's population had almost double its normal number and housing was at a premium. So we were fortunate that, after some months of searching, we came on a suitable place some three miles out of the city. It belonged to a large estate, and the tenant of many years had just died. The rent seemed more than we could afford, but we both felt we must take it, and providentially I was promoted to major on the day we moved. This gave us an extra ten shillings per day, which was a good deal of money in those days.

The Astburys, as this place was called, was a small, indeed a miniature, country house, with a gardener's cottage, many outbuildings and even a garden wall covered with fruit trees. The whole place was exceedingly well planted with flowers and produce. Half a million crocus bulbs had been placed in the lawns, which in that cold climate required no mowing till their leaves had died down! So the year's flowering began in January and continued into the late autumn with chrysanthemums. The expert gardener stayed on. He had become a member of the Observer Corps, which had to identify planes in the vicinity. But his duties allowed him considerable free time, during which he worked for us at a small hourly rate, in return for being allowed to stay rent free with his large family in the small cottage. It was an ideal arrangement for everyone and meant that we could give the children a beautiful and peaceful environment.

Oddly enough, just before we moved in, a bomb had fallen very close by, and my colonel, who had been living next door, was moving away to please his nervous wife! My first job at our new home was to clean up broken glass under the bathroom window, which had been blown out. But the war was moving into a new phase and, during the three years and more that we lived in that delectable home, there was never another air raid to disturb our peace, though we did once have a small earthquake we mistook for a 'doodle bug' bomb! Our third daughter Theodora was born at the Astburys and hardly left the extensive garden during her first two years.

I have various memories of Beatrice at that time. My mother had lent us a large picture of my father, with two sisters and a younger brother, painted lifesize in my grandfather's rock garden all dressed up in Victorian children's best clothes. When we brushed up her hair to the same shape, Beatrice's resemblance to her dead grandfather at the same age was uncanny! Another memory was Nannie Gullidge's rather than my own.

4

Jean had issued an edict that the child should only pick flowers that had fallen over, and Nannie watched from an upper window as Rowena sent smaller Beatrice down the garden path ahead of her to tread on flowers, so that they would be fallen over when she reached them! Beatrice however soon became independent and developed a good opinion of herself. She was heard one day imitating the B.B.C. "Our next item will be a violin solo. The violinist will be Beatrice Hill; the pianist will be someone no-one has ever heard of!" This was of course before she learned to play the violin, but showed perhaps the instrument she already favoured.

I remained at Western Command. Several medical boards had declared I was not fit for active duty as an infantryman because of my feet, and for some strange reason, because I had belonged briefly to an infantry territorial unit, I had to be upgraded in the infantry or not at all! By staying so long in the accommodation section, I became the type of expert who knows more and more about less and less, and so almost indispensable. But I was relieved from monotony by being made the liaison officer for accommodation purposes with the American forces, who were entering the Command in increasing numbers. Quite a few of them came to meals, bringing their excellent rations to help out. One even left his violin at our house so that he could come and practise with Jean, when he was free. It would be fanciful to suggest that meeting so many Americans early in life had any effect on Beatrice's future. But it would be true to say that from the start our children were accustomed to Americans. One very young sergeant, son of a judge in Washington, spent several leaves with us and became a real favourite with all three of them.

During these years Jean's father, Sir James Morton, died. He was a remarkable man and, insofar as heredity contributes to the abilities of descendants, I am sure that the Morton inheritance contributed a great deal to Beatrice's talents. To quote from Sir James's obituary in the *Times* newspaper: "A Scot of great driving power, with his business energy enriched by marked artistic qualities, he was bound to leave his impress on the art and craft of weaving. His dominating artistic sensitiveness and interest in science and research made him a leader in the production of fadeless fabrics, refreshingly beautiful in colour and design. It was, indeed, his outstanding service to show that in furnishing fabrics machine production and beauty

5

can go hand in hand."

I would add that Lady Morton, who lived many years longer, was also a person of great intelligence, while one of her brothers, a judge in India, was an outstanding amateur mathematician.

From my side of the family Beatrice gained, as I have already stated, some of her physical appearance, though her fine bone structure was more that of a Morton. Her musical ability could be traced both to her mother and mine, who had been educated to be a professional pianist and kept up her playing to a near professional standard throughout almost all of her long life. Jean was a cellist, as well as being a good accompanist, but her principal interest was in writing. She had more than one play performed, and published three novels as well as numerous short stories. I had been a history scholar at Oxford and later spoke a good deal in public in addition to writing. So I like to think that Beatrice's gift for expressing complex ideas in simple terms came in some degree from both parents. It was one of her great talents and responsible, I have no doubt, for her being in such demand in the last years of her life as a speaker and lecturer in Europe, America, and even farther afield.

CHAPTER TWO

Emigration and Schools in Canterbury

1945–1950

Just before the end of the war with Japan I was told when I would be 'disembodied'! Apparently I had been embodied as a Territorial officer and had to go through the opposite process to leave the army. Jean and I went to Scotland on my final leave and on a hillside there first discussed the possibility of emigrating. She did not want to leave her family, but she had never been strong and wartime shortages had affected her health. I was convinced that more sunshine and better food would make her stronger, and we were agreed that we wanted the children to grow up in a freer social atmosphere than existed in Britain in our childhood. I had another more personal reason. For I had decided not to return to the lawyer's office where I was working at the start of the war, but to be ordained. Wales was my home, but I spoke no Welsh and for that reason would be of small use in the Church in Wales. So the idea of starting my new profession in a new country had considerable appeal.

But meanwhile we returned home to Llandaff where there was a theological college. Years before I had passed the General Ordination Examination of the Church of England and only needed a refresher course, and this I could take as 'day boy.' St. Michael's College had been bombed out, but it was operating across the road in the large Victorian palace, which the bishop had gladly abandoned for a more convenient house. The palace chapel had lost all its windows from bombing, and they had been only loosely boarded up. So matins at 7.30 a.m. on a winter's morning may have been good for the soul, but was very hard on the body, even well wrapped in overcoat, scarf and gloves. It was too much for mine!

Rowena had gone to a small school where she contracted whooping cough which was caught by the other two children. Nannie Gullidge supplied bowls in the nursery in case the coughing fits led to further trouble, and I recall small Beatrice pursuing her smaller sister, Theodora, holding a bowl out in case of need. Then, before the whoops were even done with, all the children developed chicken pox and so did I! The weather was dreadful and the roof of our very old dwelling began to leak. It had been unsettled when a parachute mine, presumably meant for the Cardiff docks, had become entangled in the cathedral spire, and pieces of that roof had landed on ours at least three hundred yards distant. Jean and Nannie competed with buckets to catch the drops, and with four bedridden patients, the thought of a sunnier climate became very appealing.

British Columbia would have been our choice for a new home. Both of us had been there and had loved it. But at that time no sterling could be moved into the dollar area and the idea of arriving penniless in Western Canada with three children did not seem practicable. Then Australia became a possibility, because one of my sisters, who was working for the Wool Secretariat, was told by the High Commissioner of an Australian state of a Wakefield-like scheme for founding entire communities of immigrants, who would need chaplains to emigrate with them. I saw this man and thought the idea wonderful. But it was rather a distant prospect, and in fact never materialised. Meanwhile I had a good chance to consider New Zealand.

On returning home without George and Cissie, who had gone to help a sick friend, we turned the former dining room at Llandaff House into a kitchen and let the back of the house, which included an old billiard room. Our tenant was the Reverend Merlin Davies, who had just returned from New Zealand to be the Student Christian Movement chaplain at Cardiff University. His wife Kathleen came from Timaru, and had recently inherited a large library of books about New Zealand, including all the recent centennial volumes, published for the celebrations in 1940. I devoured these while convalescing from my severe chicken pox. Then Jean recalled that, when she was a child in Carlisle, the next door neighbour had been a canon of

8

the cathedral, who had gone to New Zealand to become bishop of Christchurch and subsequently archbishop of New Zealand. Merlin Davies had served under him and encouraged Jean to write to him. In reply Archbishop West Watson unexpectedly offered me an immediate job. We felt rushed but accepted. So, within a year of my 'disembodiment,' we found ourselves with our three daughters sailing to the other side of the world, uprooted from our old home, but not yet planted in a new.

Nannie Gullidge had to be left behind, as she did not rate priority for a passage. But she was determined to join us as soon as possible, and this proved to be after only a few months.

We arrived in Christchurch at the end of August 1946 when the spring term had started. So Rowena and Beatrice went for the rest of it to a kindergarten run by Miss Youngman, a remarkable woman who could keep order in a whole crowd of children without ever raising her voice! Her establishment was close to the furnished house which had been found for us, and which we needed to leave as soon as possible as the weekly rent was higher than my wage as a curate! Housing was in short supply after the war, but as against that house prices were controlled. So the sale of our Llandaff home enabled us to buy a large home within bicycling distance of the Merivale church where I was working. It was also close enough for Rowena and Beatrice to go to St. Margaret's diocesan school for girls, which gave special terms for clergy daughters.

Beatrice was placed in the kindergarten and the report for her second term there survives. "Her number work is excellent and her printing neat" it stated. There survives too a letter which Beatrice printed during our first summer in New Zealand when the children had gone with Nannie Gullidge to a farm by the sea at Little Akaloa on the Banks Peninsula. It is surprisingly long and clear for a child not yet quite six recording how "Theodora and I can go nice and deep in the sea with Rowena"—"Some nights Rowena and I watch the calves being fed, they are sweet. Rowena Theodora and I see the cows being milked by machines"—"Love from Beatrice." Her report for standard one a year later gave her an A for arithmetic, with the added comment "Mental excellent." Her highest marks however were for spelling, grammar and reading.

By then I was about to become vicar of Southbridge, a small country township between Lake Ellesmere and the Rakaia river. At that time it possessed a District High School with a

Primary Department, which the children attended. Beatrice's report for the year 1949 is in two halves on one form, the second showing a marked improvement over the first. As at St. Margaret's all the English subjects and arithmetic rated A's while only handwork descended to C+. "The best in the class" commented her form mistress. She had been moved up from standard three to standard four during the year, and I have no doubt the headmaster, Mr. Chapple, was to be thanked for this change. For at that time when 'social promotion' was the catch cry, meaning that an entire age group was kept in the same class almost regardless of achievement, Mr. Chapple held firmly to the belief that the worst thing that could happen to any child was to be bored at school and that clever children especially must be occupied to the full extent of talent. For Beatrice this was the best possible treatment, as her better performance in the second part of the year demonstrated. And there were no signs that promotion out of her age group did her any social harm. She was always a popular child and able to look after herself among older children.

I possess a letter of eight small pages, which she wrote to her mother on December 16th, 1948, describing a Southbridge school outing to Lyttelton harbour. "The school picnic was very nice. We went to the station and at Christchurch they changed engines. Soon after we left Christchurch we went through the tunnel. It was lovly (sic) in the launch. In the middle of the day at about $\frac{1}{2}$ past 1 the launch came and we had a ride round the coast of quail island (for 6d). At the top of quite a high bank were some ropes hanging from trees; with knots at the end, and we used them as swings by sitting on the knots. Coming back on the launch the waves kept spraying on to the ship, and in the tunnel it was dreadfully dark because the lights were not on. Daddy met us at the station, and, when we got home I had supper with Daddy.

"On Sunday night dec 12 there were 16 children after carols. (sic) We had lovely fun IN BED 10 o'clock.
Food we had chocolate biscuits,
        plane   "
        cake
        raspberry drink.
Love from Beatrice."
A good effort, I think, for a seven-year-old.

During the winter of 1949 Nannie Gullidge decided to return to England. She was not feeling well and, as she put it, wanted to "lay her bones in the old country" (an event which was to be postponed for some twenty years!)

Three months before she left, Beatrice started to write a little book entitled "My lovely Nanny" and she made periodic entries up to the time of Nanny's departure. Here is a selection: "28/6/49. I think she is the best Nanny in the world." "2/7/49 Not once has she forgotten our birthdays or Christmas." "12/7/49

A SONG ABOUT NANNY

I love my little Nanny,
I think she is so good;
She keeps us safe from any harm,
And gives us lovely food.
But now she has to leave us,
And, Oh, I am not glad
For Nanny love is going,
So of course I am so sad.
Nanny love is going
Of course I am so sad."

Spasmodic entries continued till "13/10/1949 Last night it was Nanny's last night. I had supper with her. We had bacon and eggs (this is my favourite thing) meringues and bread and butter."

At the end of the book there are a series of small prayers for Nanny. "(1) Please God keep Nanny from any harm as she had done for us—Please God give Nanny good food as she had done for us. Amen." "(2) And I pray thee now Nanny is going to leave the vicarage that she will have a happy trip to England."

Up to that time Nanny Gullidge had been possibly the most important person in Beatrice's life and she was to recall many years later the enormous sense of loss she felt on her departure. It was as well therefore that at the time she could so well record how she felt and do much to sublimate the sense of loss. Only a year later she was writing another booklet entitled "My Happiest Days."

11

CHAPTER THREE

Primary School Days, New Plymouth

1950–1953

During the following year I resigned as vicar of South-bridge to go to help my friend the Reverend J. T. Holland, who had recently become vicar of New Plymouth and badly needed assistance in his large parish. I had enjoyed living in South-bridge with the wonderful trout and salmon fishing and the friendly people. But I could not think I was fulfilling my vocation there. Also the Canterbury plain in winter turned out to be nearly as cold as the climate we had left for Jean's health. So a move north was indicated, and New Plymouth, which had greatly attracted me when I was reading Kathleen Davies' books about New Zealand, was a place where we felt at home from the moment we got there.

The children went to the central primary school and Beatrice continued to benefit from Mr. Chapple having promoted her by continuing in a form commensurate with her abilities. No reports on her work at this school have survived and she was to say later that she did not think it was outstanding. There survives, however, a description of her activities at home at this time, which Jean sent to her mother, Lady Morton. It is reproduced below.

BEATRICE March 1951

"Beatrice is ten, short, burly, rosy-faced, with big sparkling hazel eyes and brown hair whose natural state is one of extreme dishevelment. Her nose is of the 'baby beak' variety, finely chiselled, and her mouth small and firmly set.

"Beatrice is always either up or down, mostly up, fortunately for those with whom she lives. When clouds come up, they gather and a storm is inevitable. It may be a long and noisy storm. Nearly always it happens when some creative project, whether it be one of her many 'Heath Robinson' contraptions or only some elaborate 'pretend,' has been frustrated or interrupted.

"From the moment she wakes at six a.m. or earlier she is busily involved. Seven is the earliest she is allowed to get up and dress, but that doesn't mean she can't put in a good hour's concentrated work on something she has on hand. Music comes first. Sometimes it seems as though she thinks in music. No need for Beatrice to be actually playing one of her instruments, piano or violin, to be making music. All she knows of theory, note values, chords, phrases, rhythm has to be passed on to Bruce.

"Meet Bruce. He is a wooly koala, rather dull to the uninitiated observer, but mildly benevolent and patient in expression, as indeed he needs to be, because he endures much, much tuition, much imparting of every kind of knowledge, at all times of day not spent by his owner at school. 'Bruce Brown' is taught by 'Muriel Green': Beatrice's room is littered with papers which testify to the thoroughness with which he is taught. Her mother and father feel they might learn quite a lot of the rudiments of musical theory if they could only steal Bruce's M.S. book from time to time and study it. Some of the instructions are: 'Write the scales, chords and inversions as directed'—'Put in bar lines'—'Also write the time signature'—'Name the key of the following'—'Write the following in the same position on the treble staff. Prefix the new key signature.' There are numerous headings and sub-headings: 'Theory. 1st Examination'—'Theory 2nd Examination'—'Hints and Rules'—'Memoranda.' Nothing is copied. It is all out of her own head.

"Now meet the Rubapluc, an instrument made and invented by Beatrice and played by Bruce. While Beatrice is in bed, before or after lying-down-hours, he can be seen perched up with music in front of him on the folding music stand, clutching his harp-like instrument and being patiently instructed in its use. It took hours to make the Rubapluc. It is kept in a cardboard box, neatly covered with Christmas paper. On the outside is a label saying 'This is a box containing a WONDERFUL RUBAPLUC instrument and Bupluk.' The latter is the metal top of a coat-hanger. It lives in a slot in the lid and is used to twang the strings. The idea is a wooden frame, shaped most ingeniously, through which go wooden posts, a rubber band going above and below each, so that there are six strings and each makes a definite note on the piano, which is marked on the cardboard beside each. Bruce has his own music. Chords can be played by twanging two strings at once and are written in the music provided, or single lines of nursery rhymes can be picked out.

"On a brief tour round Beatrice's small room the following were discovered:

1) A carefully written double sheet of a school notebook 'Ballet Grade 1.' Full description of different positions and dances (all original) with pin-figures to illustrate it.

2) A large sheet with much coloured lettering 'Second Examination! Give the meaning of the following'—with many musical signs and marks allocated accordingly.

3) A piece of cardboard with a design of triangles—'How many are there?' Very elaborate calculations and diagrams to find the result.

4) A sheet of paper about 4 ft. by 2 ft. covered with divisions, each containing written out instructions in large childish printing (not her normal writing) for the music lessons of other members of the koala family, Big Rookie, Ann, Stripie, Teddy and Wee Rookie, with comments—'Fair work'—'Good'—'Count out loud'—etc.

5) An odd sheet of music MS with coloured notes and huge gold stars at intervals. (Purpose—who knows?)

6) A small box containing two bottles of home-made scent, with 'Shake a drop. Grand Double rose and lavender' printed on the outside.

7) Several cardboard lids with shells held down by transparent cellophane paper, neatly numbered and named.

"Her room generally in a normally untidy state, but the things she had actually made are characterised by neatness, originality and ingenuity.

"To Beatrice, engaged in some of her private operations, meals and requests to wash her hands or get ready for bed are obviously nothing more nor less than tiresome interruptions. Grown-ups are intruders and the ordinary grown-up world another country.

"She goes into protracted day-dreams and is interestingly absent minded. One evening when she seemed to be undressing more slowly than usual, with long dreamy intervals of doing nothing, her mother was delighted to see that at last she at least had on her pyjama tops. Not long afterwards Beatrice wandered into her mother's room without them and only the trousers on. 'Mummy' she said in a rather worried way, 'I know I had my tops on, but now they're off again.'

"The first occasion on which she was allowed to walk home

alone from her violin lesson (not more than fifteen minutes walk) she turned up after forty-five minutes in the dark, twenty of them having been spent in anxious surmise by both her family and her violin teacher. When she wandered in, blissfully happy and dreaming, she couldn't understand what all the fuss was about and said she hadn't done anything on the way. She 'just came.'

"A very familiar sight is Beatrice at the piano, with Bruce alongside high on a cushion on another chair, being given a lesson. Original little themes and phrases are used as she goes along. Occasionally one of them seems to please her. It is repeated over and over again, and now a large musical MS book she has been given is being used to write out these little musical ideas. They are fully harmonised, and generally illuminated with coloured pictures and figures round the edge.

"Non-musical 'pretends' are always elaborate and thorough—picnics, cinema shows, school, everything for the 'creatures,' with Theodora as faithful collaborator. If the news gets round that it's Bruce's birthday today, or Teddy is to have his tonsils out, everyone knows that at least half a day is going to be blissfully happily spent. All that is asked of mere grown-ups is to keep out of the way."

Mostly indoor pursuits, however, were not the whole story, as is shown by the illustrated volume "My Happiest Days," to which I have already referred. The introduction reads: "The reason why I wrote this book is because, when I came back from Pony club on the 14th of October, I was so grateful for all the things that happened that I decided I must write them down."

We had owned ponies at Southbridge, where there was a paddock belonging to the vicarage, but it was Rowena rather than Beatrice who had enjoyed riding them. Probably they were too large for her, and it was the smaller pony we bought in New Plymouth which turned her for a while into an enthusiastic rider. "My Happiest Days" was dedicated to "Jimmy because I will never love a pony more than I have loved him." It contains nine chapters of which the following is chapter three.

An all-day birthday picnic. 21st October 1950

"One day as I entered the dining room to set the table for breakfast I saw an extraordinary note on the table! This is how it read. Had breakfast taken lunch and gone. See you at five p.m. Rowena.

"In the middle of breakfast the telephone bell rang. It was Rowena saying she had gone for an all-day ride and that I could come too. I wondered how I could come when we only had one pony. I asked her. She replied saying that Annette Giles could not come on Pete (her pony) unless another pony called Gipsy came too. Judy would ride Gipsy and I would ride Paul. I ate some breakfast. Mummy cut me some lunch. When I arrived at the Browns' place, Mrs. Brown told me that the others had already gone up to the paddock to bring the ponies up here. They soon arrived leading Paul. The name of Barbara Brown's pony is Hexy, Judy was not there as she had gone up with Annette to her paddock to fetch Gipsy and Pete. So Rowena, Barbara and I set off to Margaret McAllan's paddock to meet her. We found her there and after some wait Judy and Annette came. Then we all went to fetch Jane Ward and her pony Dinah. These are everybody who went; Rowena on Jimmy; Me on Paul; Judy on Gipsy; Jane on Dinah; Annette on Pete; Barbara on Hexy and Margaret on Billy. We were going to a farm near Spotswood owned by Mr. Dobson. It was a very nice ride to the farm, and when we arrived there we jumped over a post and rail for a short while. Then Mr. Dobson directed us to the place we wanted for a picnic. As it was not quite lunch time when we arrived, we had some fun. To cut a long story short after lunch we played for a bit, and then we had a game of Cowboys and Indians. The latter was a good game until everybody had got thorns in their feet! On the way back we gave the ponys (sic) a drink, but Paul wanted more, so he went straight under a tree with low branches. (I did not know he was going under the tree till I banged my head on a branch). I don't know what would have happed (sic) if I had not had my riding hat, but at any rate I had a headache on the way home."

The final chapter departed from the equestrian theme. Dated 25 Dec. 1950 it lists in most orderly fashion the presents found in her stocking and round the Christmas tree, as well as the food she ate: "Two large helpings of roast turkey,—one of plum pudding (I didn't get a threepence) and one of meringues and fruit salad." "At tea there was a lovely cake with green icing." This entry is in ink and must have been written next day, for it ends "I went to sleep happily that evening, thinking of the past day."

Certainly Beatrice was a busy and happy child. But she was by no means altogether placid. When frustrated she could roar! A notable example of this characteristic occurred when she found that one of the elastic bands on the WONDERFUL RUBAPLUC had perished and she could not retune it. Her anguish was prolonged, loud and wholehearted!

About that time she acquired the nickname Beetle, which

was to stick to her the rest of her life among the family. I have a birthday card addressed to "Poppikins from your pet Beetle Bug." It contains three sets of original verses with marginal decorations and on the back is written "I am the only beetle who can draw and make up poems." It must be admitted that the verses were not as good as those of her sister Rowena, whose later poems in Spanish and English have been published. But Beatrice did occasionally have flashes of originality, as shown by her reaction in verse to a new 'perm' of her mother's. I set it out as nearly as possible in the shape of the manuscript.

MA'S HAIR

Ma went
To Town

         (When she came back)

We bent
Right down

         (So we couldn't see this Lydee!)

Her hair
Was tight

         (So tight it was hard)

To bear
Such a sight.

More conventional was an ode entitled "Early Morning," recording what she could see from her window. The second verse began

I see the dainty blue sea lightly tipped with foam
Over these wide waters I'd some day like to roam.

It was a wish to be amply fulfilled in years to come, flying to so many astronomical schools and meetings across the Atlantic and the Pacific oceans, and a first overseas flight came unexpectedly soon.

Jean and I had a considerable and most unexpected windfall, and we decided that, if the parish and school would give us permission, we would take the children to see the family in Britain. The grannies, especially Lady Morton, were aging, and we did not want our children to lose touch with their British cousins. So we flew 'home' via San Francisco and Canada. In those days air travel was more leisurely. Our trans-Pacific flight actually included sleeping bunks on the way to Honolulu, as well as a day there at the airline's expense! There the children were specially delighted to be garlanded free of charge with real orchids (not the plastic variety which greets tourists today). Then a day and a night in San Francisco allowed time for a drive across the bridge to the Muir woods, and on an afternoon in Vancouver I recall taking the children to the large Hudson Bay store, while their mother rested. I kept 'losing' them going opposite ways on moving staircases which they had never seen before! One of my brothers was in Ottawa at the time in the British High Commission, and as there was not room for all of us in his flat, Beatrice and I were boarded out with remote relatives he had discovered. Beatrice was delighted to find that shuffling across their luxurious carpets and touching someone produced a spark and a sharp shock! I had experienced this odd phenomenon on a pre-war visit to Ottawa and I do not know how often it occurs. But discovering it was naturally a thrill for a child with a scientific bent, and not even our host, a retired general, was spared an occasional surreptitious attack!

In Britain, the children stayed mostly with my mother, and the family album contains happy pictures of them with her horses and dogs.

Beatrice alone paid a visit to London to stay with her godmother, my sister Patsy. A letter of seven large pages describes the visit. It starts "Dear Mummy, I am having a gorgeous time. (Whoopee). Grandma put me in a compartment next to the Guard's van and my case was with the guard."

Nannie Gullidge met the train at Paddington and took her former charge to the Derry and Toms roof garden. After work my sister Patsy collected her, and, when they had had "supper," they took a taxi to Battersea Park, which Beatrice called the Pleasure Gardens and Fun Fair.

"When we got there," she wrote, "the lights were not lit but it was all very pretty. The fountains are simply beautiful. We soon wandered over to the fun fair and the first thing we did was to go on the Emmet Railway which was awfully funny. Then we got tickets for a racing car and motor bike show on a wooden track, but we waited so long hearing they would start in two minutes that we gave up and had an exiting (sic) trip through the Grand Canyon on the Senic (sic) railway. We kept thinking we would bump our heads as we whizzed through a downhill tunnel in the canyon. Then we went on the BIG

DIPPER!!!!!!!!! It is super. Aunty Patsy had never dared to go on it before, but I made her. You sit in a little car with people in front of you and behind you and set off along the rails. You just get going nice and fast when you climb a steep hill for what seems ages and then you suddenly see below you the rails and you jerk forward (screaming) and whoosh down leaving your inside behind you. Then you do three *slightly* smaller dips running and then another two. Then you do a very little one and stop. Aunty Patsy and I stayed on for another turn, which was lovely too. After that we had a toboggan. You sit in a comfy chair and go round and round like a caterpiller. Then I drove Aunt Patsy round in a bumper car. There was a notice saying no speed limit, so we accelerated all the time. The annoying part was that you suddenly all went backwards on the same speed for a moment. Then we quietened ourselves with a tree-top walk. Then I had a lovely lighted ride on a little Welsh pony and soon had another. Then we walked round the luminous fountains and saw the Guiness clock striking quarter to eleven. By then most of the amusements had closed, but I managed to make Aunt Patsy have two more rides on the Big Dipper. Then we took a taxi home and I went straight to bed and had a drink and biscuit in bed."

Next morning they set off to see the changing of the guard in Whitehall. "The horses are enormouse (sic), and they rode past so close I could have patted them. Afterwards we talked to one of the horses on guard."

Next day shopping at Hamleys, the toy shop, was followed by a water bus ride on the Thames and a visit to the theatre. "Fuzzy" (my sister's friend Mrs. Dewhurst) "came for supper in the evening and after supper she drove us in the Bentley to the (sorry I've forgotten the name and I've packed my programme) theatre. The play was 'Call me Madam.' It was screamingly funny but gorgeous music and dancing. The theatre was frightfully posh, and even provided glasses for looking at the stage. The main star was Billie Worth as Mrs. Sally Adams or Madam. I could write pages about it so I won't start on the story. On the way back through Piccadilly Circus and Trafalgar Square and till we were home I sat on the back of the front seat with my head out of the roof. It certainly got rid of the stuffiness of the theatre!" The letter ends "Love from Beetle. P.S. I do sit down sometimes."

After this exciting visit my sister and Fuzzy decided that

20

Beatrice was destined for the stage, but I do not think that idea ever entered her head. I have a vivid memory of Beatrice in La Guardia airport on our way back to New Zealand. We had been visiting friends in New York and it was tremendously hot. For some reason the air conditioning had broken down in the place where we had a long wait for our plane to Los Angeles. We all became restless except our Beetle, who was sitting quietly on a high stool with a cold drink in front of her calmly bringing her 'trip book' up to date. She was ten and a half years old.

CHAPTER FOUR

New Plymouth Girls High School

1953–1957

Back in New Plymouth I was given charge of the three small churches at the west end of the parish. We went to live near the harbour, and soon afterwards Beatrice joined her elder sister, Rowena, at the Girls High School.

One day Jean drew my attention to a timetable stuck to the wall above Beatrice's bed. It was divided in squares for each hour of the day on each day of the week. Those not to be spent at school were carefully allotted to music practice or play or homework, and this was the first of many such timetables, which were adhered to with discipline. They were entirely Beatrice's own idea and it was not surprising that Rose Allum, the remarkable headmistress at the High School, commented later that she had been the perfect student.

This did not keep her from enjoying the allotted 'play' times. We were near to the safe and sandy Ngamotu beach, which has since been swallowed up by harbour works, and in summer many 'play' times were spent there. I recall others with Beatrice and Theodora on the front lawn trying at great length, though not with great success, to teach our small corgi to do circus tricks! Riding was not entirely forgotten but it was soon abandoned. We found nowhere close to our new home where we could keep ponies and, with homework increasing, there was less time to fetch and ride them. More time was also needed for violin lessons with Willi Komlos and practising for the school orchestra.

Beatrice's high school reports, of which I still have the majority, make almost monotonous reading. She gained consistently high marks in all subjects and won her form prize each year! In the first year her best subjects were Latin, Science and French, with violin playing described as "Excellent." In the second year mathematics took over from science in the top group, though science remained "excellent." Violin playing was "making excellent progress." In the third year she won cups for Latin, mathematics and speech, and every one of her subjects was described as very good or very good indeed.

At the end of that year Rose Allum came to call on us. Rowena had previously gained one of the top ten Junior scholarships for New Zealand and Rose was convinced that Beatrice could do the same if she would continue with her English. But Beatrice did not agree. She was determined to do more mathematics. So Rose not only gave way, but made special arrangements. No girl had done scholarship maths at the school for over twenty years, but fortunately one of the staff, Miss Alma Davis, was qualified to take part of the course. For the rest Beatrice went to the Boys High School, and at the end of the year she gained her Junior scholarship, in seventh place out of the ten. Looking back I can see that she displayed considerable character not only in her determination to do mathematics for the scholarship but in the disciplined way she had concentrated on her studies during all her high school years. Our family life had undergone a big change, which could have been unsettling. For during her second year at high school I was elected mayor of New Plymouth and Jean published a novel which had a wide circulation in New Zealand. So the family had come in for considerable local publicity and, as mayor and mayoress, Jean and I were much more often away from home. However, I cannot recall that any of this deflected Beatrice from her own disciplined way of life.

When she left the High School Beatrice was not quite seventeen and I do not recall how she first met a young man from Auckland, who came to stay with us at our bach on Lake Taupo at her request during the summer holidays. He was good looking and charming, with a considerable sense of humour and a gift for acting which led to his taking the lead soon afterwards in one of New Zealand's first feature films. We had a taste of this gift when he pretended successfully for several days to be

24

an American from Texas and totally deceived the young English-man with whom he shared a tent! He gave up finally because he felt he was being cruel. We had a lot of fun with him on that holiday, but it was a shock when he and Beatrice informed us they were engaged! The romance lasted till the following May during Beatrice's first vacation from Canterbury University. The young man then came to New Plymouth to partner her at the high school debutante ball. After that the engagement faded out, though I do not know just how or when. He was a youth of many talents. To this day a highly imaginative 'moonscape' of his adorns one of the family homes. It is well executed in acryl-ic paints, though I am not sure that he ever had formal art les-sons. But, for all his abilities, he and Beatrice were definitely not well suited. Her genius, if her considerable gifts amounted to that, conformed to Newton's definition of an infinite capacity for taking pains, whereas he took life at a gallop, expecting to clear all its fences with no time-consuming preparations.

Whatever she may have felt when the engagement ended, I can find no sign that Beatrice was deeply upset. It is possible, of course, that her mother destroyed letters relating to what could have been a painful subject, but in those which survive there is only one passing reference to the young man. Instead they show clearly that Beatrice was entering enthusiastically into student life at Canterbury University.

CHAPTER FIVE

Canterbury University

1958–1963

A few days after the start of her first term at Canterbury Beatrice explained why she was already finding university study such an enormous stimulus.

"Dear Family," she wrote, "I'm meant to be attending to a bloke who's lecturing on the trig we've all known for two years, so I'm writing this to save myself from going to sleep.—Pure maths is rather a farce, and at present so is applied but that'll improve as we advance. Physics is really super. Doc. Gregory is a most interesting lecturer and goes frequently into the philosophical reasons for knowing anything anyway it's miles more satisfactory than learning strings of facts in an orderly manner and never knowing why anyone knows it. His first lecture was a long discussion on 'What is Science?, what is real?, what is length?, what is being? etc. etc. and going into the attitude towards learning being building everything up from experiment, *not* using the theories we've been taught to see if an experiment 'worked.' In other words doing the very opposite from the unbearable school attitude. Now we're starting on the subject of measurement, going into how man perceives length and how it's measured, and today it was 'time' which was terrific. Wonderful training in taking nothing for granted. It's our job to try to prove a theory wrong rather than assuming it's right. Everything must be thought of from a logical and perfectly basic beginning.

"In Chemistry its much the same; we begin from an historical point of view and learn how the theories were built up. At school we learnt up theories and saw how the experimental knowledge was explained by them, and then (to quote our lecturer) said 'That's nice!' Well here we see how the theories were thought of, then built up or discarded, *starting* with experimental evidence; which makes a stimulating atmosphere for working in. (End of lecture thank goodness). (Afternoon) The result is that I now can't look at any 'fact' in a textbook without thinking 'How did someone come to believe that? And if I had the same evidence would I believe it?' So I'm learning to question *everything*. I realise that all advances in science have been made by people who have thought along totally unconventional lines and haven't been misled by the authority of a Great Name having said it was true. Just to think that because Aristotle said things were true, so many centuries passed before someone said they weren't. Now we learn things that Newton and such Great Names have claimed as true, but why shouldn't we question them? Well the fact is we can and do, and we're constantly reminded that in science a theory is accepted only as long as it isn't disproved by experimental evidence. I doubt people would mind what theories or questions anyone liked to put forward here if they felt like it. It gives one the courage to think originally, and that is the beginning of research. Of course I've known in theory for a long time how all this is, but marvellous to be in a position to think and experiment *myself*."

There are two more pages of this long letter dealing with other matters, such as hoping to find a more congenial roommate in her women's hostel and asking for papers needed for entering for a higher grade music exam. Then follows a description of the orientation programme which culminated in an informal dance.

"I can now rock and roll after a style. It's super fun. Had some reasonable partners, then got stuck with a History Honours bloke who was dull and had no sense of rhythm and it was dretful (sic). However that was made up for by a very amusing and entertaining Engineering student (4th year) by the name of Ernie, so by the time the evening was ended I'd had a pretty good time. Why is male company so much better than endless females? Perhaps a reaction to living here. In all our lecture classes, which are well over a hundred, there are no more than ten girls. In pure maths (my particular class) there are three girls! Very nice state of affairs—for us that is."

By the following month music was absorbing a good deal of Beatrice's time. Dr. Metcalf, her inspiring chemistry lecturer, was a violinist and held chamber music sessions in his home. "Last night to the Metcalfs again" Beatrice wrote. "It's a regular now. We're learning a gorgeous Schumann piano quartet which is going to take a lot of work on my part; and also we're going to rake in Angela Connell and do the Schumann piano quintet. Also Dr. M. and I played the Bach double concerto which was great fun. Tonight I'm out violin-ing again, this time the other quartet which is setting itself up to do other things for fun."

She was writing during applied Maths. "The lecturer waffles and waffles and it takes a terrific effort to concentrate through it all in order to extract the facts. As you see I'm not trying today." Next day, after an evening of "quartet practice with the boys" she continued, "Do I ever have time to work, now I do music at least four nights a week? I'm terribly lucky aren't I?—This is really a wonderful life, full of science and labs and music. Love to you all." The signature is a drawing, meant to be a beetle.

During April Lady Morton died. She had recently written to her granddaughter and evidently knew that the end was near, for Beatrice quoted her as having stated, "You mustn't be anxious about me old self, but of course the strongest minded ma can't last for ever and wherever I am, in this world or the next, I know I shall be able to keep hovering round you." Beatrice wrote to sympathise with her mother and added, "I think it must be about the most wonderful thing of all to look back when you're near death, to think of your children and to know that because you were a mother there is no possible end to the influence of your own life."—"I'm sure both your parents are now very close to you as you sit in grandpa's chair. I'm longing to be with the family in the holidays. Last night there was a terrific howling storm and I was sitting by the fire feeling the same feelings as a little girl who is safe at home where no harm can come to her, while outside the awful wind roars but has no effect. Home is really people not places outside of one, but it is too a place inside, tho' that place can be awfully hard to find in a bustling independent life. It will be lovely to belong at home again and not in an impersonal hostel."

Later that evening, however, her mind reverted to her stud-

29

ies and she continued: "Every day I get more and more thrilled with science. The other night at the Metcalfs I spent ages talking with the Doc. (and David Buckingham) about chemistry and physics. Gosh he's (i.e., Doc. M.) an interesting person. He was telling me about various living scientists of most outstanding insight and ingenuity, who are working on different things now and the work they've done recently—all revolutionary ideas and results. Dr. M. is totally fascinated by it all himself—it sort of pours from him as he speaks—and he talks and talks about all the discoveries and says 'Isn't it thrilling?'. I do agree! He sees science as it really is and not as a mere 'subject.' I told him I thought it was a pity the way stage one had to skim over all sorts of atomic things or learn half accurate explanations for them, and he quite agreed and told me all sorts of things about the way he had to adjust his lecturing technique so that he can teach over-simplified things without letting us think that they are sufficient. I also let forth a lot of things about how maddening it was (a) to have to learn the dry sides of physics that would have no bearing on an atomic Scientist's career, and (b) to have to do such ghastly easy maths—all of which he explained why it had to be so. He doesn't care in the least about degrees and exams. etc; he only cares about knowledge. I'm therefore feeling very revolutionary and I'm damned sick of working for exams. Consequently I'm going to put first things first and instead of listening to Mr. —— waffling thru' applied maths that I did last year, or —— mumbling thru' calculus I did in 6b, I'm going to sit in the back in lectures and work on stuff that's going to get me somewhere, namely learning *new* maths. Also instead of just sticking to the syllabus work in Chem and Physics I'm reading and learning as much as I can about everything. Obviously there's no chance of doing any original work until one has a wide background of present knowledge and a *very* wide knowledge of maths. So here I go. Even if I never achieve any of my aims, I'll at least have had the thrill of knowing where I want to go—along those lines that is. And the same applies to all parts of life—it's the wanting that matters, and having a definite goal ahead. Even if one has about ten thrilling goals it hardly matters! One thing I certainly know, because I'm a woman my home must come before my science. That is right and it must be so and it would be unbearable otherwise. How bleak and bare life would be."

In mid-winter Beatrice went up to Arthur's Pass with a

group of friends. They spent one morning "careering round on hired sledges" and then she "walked miles over the Pass road, all alone amid the stillness."—"Just as well my lungs were full of fresh air, as when we got back to the hut, Nita and I shut ourselves in the kitchen and made dinner of all the remaining food well flavoured with kerosene. Talk about smoke and fumes! Next time we're at the bach I can treat you to another kind of Arthur's Pass hash; i.e., tip over a Primus so the peas get into the kero, and decide they're still edible. They aren't."

The following weekend a ball was held at the hostel. "The whole place was decorated Chinese style—paper lanterns over all the lights and incense burning in the common rooms and beautiful japonica branches on the walls—bamboo (stolen from the park) round all the messy outside passages—looked lovely. My black stole inspired me to get a large black rose to decorate my deb frock, so went all in black and white.—I had a wonderful time."

Jean and I decided to go and see our families in Britain again during the following northern summer. We took Theodora with us and, as Rowena was in Australia on her way to Italy, Beatrice was to be the only member of the family left in New Zealand. Before we left we saw her off on the ferry from Wellington to Lyttelton and, far from being dismayed at the prospect of being left alone, she was thrilled to be returning to Christchurch before the start of the university term to pursue her own studies without distraction.

Her self-reliance was soon tested. She had taken a lease on a flat in Colombo Street for six months and spent her first two days back in Christchurch in scrubbing it out. "I felt like an old rag outside" she wrote, "but terrific joyous inside 'becos' it's looking lovely." But a few days later she recorded in her diary letter: "the landlord has been getting grumpier and grumpier since his wife went into hospital last Friday and half the things he should have done before I moved in weren't done." Each time she asked for something he replied with "the same long speech about 'look-here-I'm-that-worried-about-my-wife-I-can't-do-anything.'" Finally he refused even to fix a light switch and a window. "I lost my temper" she wrote, whereupon he told her to get out, and when she reminded him of the six months lease, he stalked off calling her a perfect pest. "My hackles was up. I jolly well determined to get another flat and not pay another week's rent."

So she answered an advertisement for a flat in Shakespeare Road where the landlord's own solicitor described him as a "character who writes endless and muddled letters about letting his place." He "laughed like anything about the ad which apparently had little connection with his last instructions." Then he warned Beatrice that several people had turned down the flat because of the confusion and rather unusual decor. However she liked it and determined to take it. But, after she had moved out of Colombo St. and all her goods were loaded on the Metcalf's car, the Shakespeare Rd. landlord changed his mind and she was left spending the night on a settee in another flat in the Colombo St. house with a kind old couple, who actually gave her breakfast in bed.

"Aren't people wonderful things?" she commented. "Every time one gets to a sort of catastrophe someone comes to the rescue."

Finally the eccentric landlord changed his mind and she moved into Shakespeare Road with her friend Nita. As it turned out, when he arrived in person, he was not the least formidable. "He is small shy and tries very earnestly to please. He is terribly kind and nice and is only describable as a perfect dear."

With her housing problem settled, Beatrice turned to the question of her courses for the year. On March 1st she wrote: "I went to see Prof. Lawden on Wednesday and he was very interested and helpful: he said that my maths. were certainly unusually high, but I told him it was all a second year of the same stuff and that I'd done nearly no work on the same. He laughed and said "Nevertheless." So he said was I interested in theoretical or practical physics, and the answer's theoretical, which is of course applied Maths and not Physics. Even the highest theoretical chemists probably haven't seen a test tube in their life. *But* higher maths is a really tough philosophical and logical subject (i.e., the pure maths necessary) with nothing to do with Stage One. He said unless I really am interested in maths I'd be a fool (my word not his) to take on the maths honours course. All the same, if I'm the type that must have *proofs* for formulae etc, I'd find Physics quite unsatisfying. And, if it comes to doing one and picking up the other, I'd be wiser to do the maths while I can get the tuition. The trouble with me just now is that I want *both*: the maths to reason with and the physics to apply it to. Consequently I've left it open by enrolling for

Pure and Applied Maths Two and Physics Two, without tying myself to the honours course in either. I've put physics as my major subject, but that has no bearing on anything except to make some of the physics Dept. blink. Mary Veitch is also doing physics two, so we'll have a wonderful time—That physics dept. has been exclusively male for years now, of course apart from Stage One (which has labs in a different building). Dr. Gregory is pleased with my course. Colin Keay just stared. The chemists, i.e., Sally Page and Dr. Metcalf, tell me I'm a traitor. Anyway I'm enrolled. The week is twenty hours: 2 or 3 lectures every morning, and 2 lots of labs from 2 till 6: Thursday will be terrific: three lectures starting at 9 a.m. (imagine that in the winter), then labs from 2 to 6, then orchestra etc. afterwards. Friday is similar, but maybe (maybe) I'll be in on Friday nights.

"Music. Mr. Ritchie has said 'Soon Beatrice I want to have a little discussion with you on how much time you'll have to spend on music this year.' Answer is obvious; *Little*. (But I'll spend a lot.)" This proved true, for, apart from Dr. Metcalf's fortnightly chamber music session, she continued with the student quartets and the University orchestra. On top of that she sent in an application for an audition for the National Youth Orchestra, "chiefly becos it seemed fate that I received the form (after all the delays in forwarding) on the day it had to be in Wellington. I rang 3YA (the local radio station) and said What hope? and they said Send it direct with an explanatory note, becos anyway it was Saturday and they wouldn't be opening the entries till Monday."

The programme for the year seemed full enough, but after a music session at the Metcalfs there was "a very interesting discussion over supper"—"When Dr. M. heard what my course was he said 'That won't stretch you at all; you must do German as well,' and I'd rather be overstretched than flabby."

The good doctor also advised her "if time could be found" to take a W.E.A. course in Russian later in the year, "since German and Russian are both necessary for reading scientific literature." Beatrice took the first part of his advice and gained a pass in Science German that year. But, though she was later to collaborate with a Russian scientist, I have found no record that she ever tried to learn Russian.

The long letter of March the first had started with the statement that there was little time to write, but finally stretched to sixteen pages, including a description of the new flat and its furnishings! These included my old teddy bear, which the girls had requested as a 'chaperone' for boy friends' visits! He was up on a cupboard and Beatrice assured me "He looks very happy."

Finally, before the year's study began in earnest, it was necessary to buy books, and for the type of course Beatrice was doing they were expensive. "I've spent £ 15 and haven't got the lot yet! but £ 3 of that is a book with Aunty Helen's money." (Aunty Helen was Mrs. Hannay, a sister of Jean's and her other godmother.) "I know I was going to spend it on a record, but then I saw in the Varsity book shop this *gorgeous* book for 58s/6d and I *had* to get it. It's an American book and therefore beautiful, called 'Theories of the Universe,' and is a collection of writings from Plato to Einstein and Bondi, wonderfully put together and arranged, and being historical it won't date. One could more or less add to it oneself."

In view of Beatrice's later achievements that last sentence was perhaps prophetic! But all she added at the time was "I'm thrilled and dying to read it; 425 pages of small print."

Three weeks later a further seventeen pages dealt almost entirely with music. She was certain she had failed in her audition for the youth orchestra (she was mistaken), but had been elected onto the committee of the University Music Society. When the elections seemed finished "Mr. Ritchie said of course if anyone thinks they'd like to put a bomb under the orch. and tell them they're lazy hounds, they can nominate themselves. Immediately a voice (not mine) says 'I nominate Beatrice Hill.' Goodness knows why they think I can put bombs under the orchestra, but it's a flattering reputation to have."

Science and music were equal enthusiasms at that time. By herself on Good Friday, she wrote: "Great joy and beauty— soaring peaks of perfection—utterly inextinguishable. Am listening to the Emperor Concerto, that's why. (borrowed record). And just to think next Thursday I'll be hearing and seeing Andor Folles and the Nat. Orch. do it! What a life!"

At the end of one long letter filled with music, Beatrice was afraid she'd given a wrong impression and wrote: "I suppose you get the impression I'm not doing any work at all. But actually I *am* very absorbed in it all and working hard when I do work, which is enough of the time, and there's no point in me telling you how thrilling electronics is or Lagrange's formula or something like that becos it wouldn't get you far. Maybe it might get me somewhere some day."

We were still in Britain when she wrote her next letter from Wellington, where she had joined the other seventy-seven members of the youth orchestra. She was "loving every minute of it," both the music itself and staying with the Saunders family in Kelburn, where there was no "sticky conversation"! The practices consisted of three hours each morning, with a ten minute break for "morning cuppa (*V. welcome*)," and a further two hours in the afternoon. They were followed by "some sort of informal concert for an hour." Her place was at the back of the first violins and to start with she found bits of Beethoven's first symphony "rather beyond me." But rehearsals with the conductor John Hopkins were "super." "Also there's Bill Walden Mills and Dr. Nalden, who have been taking us for sectional practice; both slave drivers and perfectionists. Same bar over and over and over, then the next two bars, then back to letter H, then all over again—The result is that I can now play the impossible bits and the rest of the orchestra likewise." Vincent Aspey, leader of the National Orchestra, took a couple of tutorial classes for the first violins. Beatrice described him as "like a good natured Hoffnung character," very much "Take it easy, you can do it— eh?" But she learned a lot from his tutorials.

What with concerts and social life on top of orchestra practice, it was hardly surprising that by Sunday she was going to bed early as soon as she finished writing "even though we got up at ten thirty in the morning. I want to be fit when I get back to Christchurch for some solid mental work."

During the August vacation she stayed in Christchurch and attended a Chamber Music school, finding the standard rather disappointing after the youth orchestra. But she enjoyed spending time with Mrs. Metcalf and her children, while the doctor was at a conference in Perth. "The kids have positively adopted me and we have an awful lot of fun. My invention and memory are getting short of material about 'what I did when I was a little girl,' but there are a lot of lovely things I keep remembering to tell them which I'd forgotten all about."

"It's been perfect weather all this week," she wrote, "all the blossoms coming out and feeling happily spring" (sic). "The birds have started to wake up about 6 a.m.—impossible to sleep after that it seems, however late the night before! But I've discovered how to get unlimited (nearly) energy: even just 10 minutes flat on the back in total flop (mental and physical) has

35

incredible effects. Last night I had ten minutes gap in practice before the concert, so I stretched out on a table and nearly went to sleep. Good habit to develop."

Early in October we arrived home from overseas. Beatrice wrote to apologise for not ringing up, explaining that she's lost her voice. "I've been flat to the boards with xyz, and his relations, or else flat in bed with disprin and his friends."

The loss of voice etc. may well have resulted from attending a party, which she described at some length. "On Friday night there was a party which Nita and I were invited to and I decided to go rather at the last minute. It was miles away, way up Riccarton Road and we biked out with Dave against a windy wind; got there about half past nine and found it was not the kind of party we expected; most members looking as though a large quantity of drink had been consumed and very noisy and mostly jiving in a half dark and far-too-small room. All the same I was in the mood to be mad and had a gorgeous time—found I really can rock and roll not half bad with a decent partner—most partners are quite decent, if you give them the miss after a suitable time in favour of someone else! Only trouble was that my bike disappeared and I had to go home in a taxi (rather than accept various dubious offers): But the old crate turned up over a neighbour's fence in Riccarton the next morning thank goodness! One is *lost* without a bike in this world!

"Funny, looking at it objectively, how one can enjoy a hooley like that when in a detached way it seems like the lowest form of existence! By twelve o'clock, the only people who looked as tho' they were having a good time were those left jiving—others had either given up (like Dave and N) or were settled in pairs on corners of floor, sofa etc. and enough to make one sick. By the time my feet had had it I began to plan escape from the bod I was with, but fortunately the party broke up and he disappeared without much hinting; so I felt as tho' I really had a good time. All the same it doesn't add up to much does it? Lucky Nita having David to look after her and spend an evening with! There are some people who really know what they want and stick to it."

Turning abruptly to a more interesting subject, she continued: "Since I've been thinking seriously of taking physics next year I've suddenly got far more interested, perhaps the stimulating effect of talk with Professor Maclellan. Mr. Seed gave me some things to look at about Fellowships to study in other countries offered by the International Atomic Commission—by way of showing what sort of opportunities are open to a theoretical physicist. There are plenty, but one has to be really good. I'll have to wait and see how these exams turn out and anyway it'll take a lot of thought before I take on three units next year. Meanwhile I'm determined to do my ultra best to do some decent theory in exams."

During the summer vacation we all went to our bach at Hatepe on Lake Taupo and I recall Beatrice sallying forth into the bush with her violin and two clothes pegs, with which to attach her music to some convenient branch! She found it very amusing when fishermen and others came to investigate what strange bird was making the noises!

With her exam results all A's with marks in the nineties, she set herself to become a cosmologist. Evidently I did not know what the word meant, for she wrote at the start of the year's work: "D was saying, what is cosmology? Really it's theoretical astronomy; studies of theories about the universe, its origin, structure etc. (that's all!) Relativity theory is absolutely basic to it; and a lot of the work that goes on in it. I gather it is inclined to be so mathematical it gets away from 'reality'; apparently why it's necessary for me to keep up with Physics. It's hard to say what I might end up actually studying, becos when things get moving in Cosmology, the whole aspect of the subject seems to change overnight. Prof. Lawden told me that the science is due for some new advances pretty soon; I think becos a lot more observational data is being analysed.

"The fascinating thing about theoretical Physics is that you can never learn about it fast enough because there's always more being discovered to learn! And you have to specialise as soon as possible, otherwise you'll never get to the frontier of any branch of knowledge and so be able to have some new ideas."

Her decision to become a cosmologist gave her an even greater incentive to work. "Now I feel everything I learn is really getting me somewhere" she wrote, "and all useful; It's different to have *definite* aim ahead, instead of vaguely wanting to do research and not knowing *what*." She did, in fact, take three units, two in Mathematics and one in Physics. She rationed her chamber music to once a fortnight at the Metcalfs', but returned to the National Youth Orchestra for a second year. She wrote thanking us in advance for "taking on such a houseful over youth orchestra week. It really will be a glorious shambles."

My memory is not of a shambles, but of a very enjoyable party one night for some twenty members of the orchestra, when Jean and I were very impressed with the quality of the country's future musicians, a number of whom went on to become professionals.

Nita and David had become officially engaged and another close friend of Beatrice's was about to be married. She called to deliver her present and reported: "I never saw such elaborate preparations. Of course the poor girl is so tired with sewing and knitting and invitations and packing and so on, she can hardly think about anything else. Not my idea of how to prepare for a wedding—(the poor bridegroom in the background)." On coming away she teased Nita about never having enough embroidered pillow slips if she didn't get cracking "which brought forth some remark I've forgotten, but made me think I'd much rather be like her and David than —— and ——."

All of which was shortly to have very personal relevance. For by the beginning of October she herself became engaged to Brian Tinsley. "I didn't think extra comments would be needed with that photo," she wrote. "Behold two happy people. That's just how things are for now and look like staying for a while—chiefly becos I must put my exams first now. (The swot doesn't appear to be suffering any)."

This proved true, for Beatrice once more gained A's for all her exams for B.Sc.

It was no doubt a help to her that her studies and Brian's were close enough for them to be able to discuss with enjoyment several lectures by distinguished visiting scientists, which they attended together. Beatrice was so enthused by the lectures that she even tried to explain to her nonscientifically minded parents about anti-matter and cell nuclei!

Jean and I were driving to New Plymouth to fetch Theodora at the end of her last term at the high school. So we gave a lift to the engaged couple, when Brian took Beatrice to meet his parents. Rather oddly we had never met them during the seven years we lived in the city, though since then they have been real friends. Beatrice and Brian joined us at the bach on Lake Taupo later on, and I have an absurd photo of them under a large straw hat with two crowns and one brim, constructed I rather think by Theodora!

Back in Christchurch for the new term, Beatrice decided on three subjects in Physics for her M.Sc., though her letters home were not unnaturally filled with preparations for her wedding in the May vacation. One of them included an offer from four musical friends to play a quartet in the church. It is not merely trite to say she made a beautiful bride and a happy one. The reception was filled with the two families and close friends, while in attendance was old teddy! He had already attended Nita and Dave's wedding, both brides having agreed that he deserved a reward for the excellent way he had carried out his responsibilities as a chaperone!

The honeymoon was spent at Crail Bay in the Marlborough Sounds, followed by a bus trip down the west coast of the south island, returning via Arthur's Pass to Christchurch, where they went to a flat in Salisbury Street. Brian had not been awarded the fellowship he had hoped for, but Beatrice was not alarmed. "I hope it appears to you as it does to us," she wrote, "that we're quite safe financially if not exactly rolling in wealth. He heard the other day that plenty of students want coaching, and the rate is fifteen shillings an hour, generally very profitable work."

Letters are not to be found for the rest of that year, but on her twenty-first birthday on January 27th, 1962 Beatrice stated: "Work is going O.K. I am trying to do forty hours a week solid at the department, which is reasonable but means hard work, when you take the time necessary for shopping, cooking etc. every day." For the time being music seems to have been crowded out but, though her studies were not wholly congenial, she was happy.

In June came her first separation from Brian when he went to Samoa to witness, as he put it, "the very spectacular effects of a high thermonuclear explosion." He was away longer than he intended, because the Air Force flight on which he had relied for the return journey was for some reason cancelled. He came back "not much browned" and thinking they deserved a second honeymoon. But they were at once involved in a Science Congress at which he gave two papers, in spite of having an awful cold "which made him feel ghastly." Beatrice wrote "We've still nothing like caught up on all there is to communicate and feel very lucky that we can understand so much of each other." They were in fact working together to some extent; for Beatrice had become a licensed operator of the university computer, which Brian was not. So she was checking his work as well as her own, and one day wrote that she must keep her appointment with the computer even when she had caught Brian's cold, because "one's time is so limited by queues."

Back in 1960 she had forecast that her M.Sc. thesis would probably not be on anything "very astronomical, because it's not studied here." As it turned out she chose what seems to me at least an obscure topic in Physics, "Theory of the Crystal Field of Neodymium Magnesium Nitrate." For this she gained first class honours, but, as soon as the thesis was complete, was agog to return to cosmology.

Possibly because her work was not really interesting, she almost became disillusioned with research as such during that year, stating that she and Brian were both feeling they wanted to "understand as much as possible about people" and were afraid that taking up some specific line of research might cut them off from "wider usefulness in the world." But nothing more was said about this once she returned to her own line of study.

At the end of August Jean and I celebrated our silver wedding and Brian and Beatrice came to Wellington to be with us. She brought her violin, but warned her pianist sister, Theodora, that "what with being a wife again (not regretted) and school and congress and thesis, it's only been played at odd evenings of chamber music lately."

"School" was the girls' high school, where she was teaching science to senior girls. At the end of the year she wrote: "I've really enjoyed teaching this year—It's a great thing to try helping young girls on the way to the world and they are such a nice crowd. We had some awfully worthwhile discussions in the last week, as I read them some interesting books etc. on the nature of science and the job of a scientist, his responsibility to society and so on. I thought it a great pity that with most of the teachers they quite wasted the last two weeks."

Even before her thesis was finished, Beatrice had written "Big talks about possible futures, as I'm expected to hand in applications for overseas scholarships. As Dr. E. said, I can but refuse if I'm offered one to go where Brian isn't."

By then she was "feeling very cynical" as she swotted for an exam on Nuclear Physics. Brian still thought that the medical uses of power reactors had meant that they did more good than "the harm the bombs have done yet." But Beatrice could no longer imagine a limited war, though, in accordance with the belief at the time, she thought the southern hemisphere would be safe. On the morning of her exam, there was news of a megaton bomb having been exploded and Brian tried to hide the newspaper from her. But she wrote "I'd dreamt the very thing the night before, so had a look."

By mid-December she knew that she had gained first class honours for exam papers, though she was still trying to find out what was thought of her thesis. She and Brian celebrated the end of exams with dinner at a restaurant and an hour "walking around the river banks in the sunset." "It was lovely," Beatrice commented. Then, having more leisure, she went back to the chamber music evenings at the Metcalfs' and attended a splendid performance of the Messiah.

Not till after Beatrice's death, when Professor Weybourne kindly sent me a print-out of all her results at Canterbury University, did I learn that she had been awarded the Haydon prize for Physics and the Charles Cook, Warwick House, Memorial Scholarship. Another member of the staff wrote at the same time, expressing the almost incredible, if very pleasing, opinion that she had been perhaps the most brilliant student who ever attended the university.

Brian had for some while been looking for a post in the United States, but was determined that he would not take one connected with armaments. This ruled out several possibilities, but eventually, not long after they returned to Christchurch at the start of the term at the Girls school where Beatrice continued teaching, she told us: "Another place has arisen to which Brian and I are putting our feelers, the Southwest Center for Advanced Studies, in Dallas, Texas! Dr. Ellyett was sent some flashy looking literature about this place, which is setting up a big new lab for Earth and Planetary Sciences and would apparently welcome people like Brian. So he (Dr. E.) has written away on our behalf, also to enquire if they could use someone at my level who is interested in relativity theory, which is part of the theoretical side of the outfit. Sounds exciting and great for a year or two! Imagine Brian under a Sombrero and talking with a Texan drawl! But I'd be surprised if we stayed there long."

After that events moved quickly and by the end of March Brian had accepted a job at the Center and they were talking of leaving New Zealand by September.

As it turned out it was to be no temporary stay for Brian, who over twenty years later is still a valued professor at what was the Center and is now part of the University of Texas at Dallas.

It was not till July that Beatrice knew that the Grants Committee, apparently under some pressure from Professor Lawden, had agreed to her holding her scholarship at the Southwest Center. Brian, whose thesis on a spectrometer was barely finished, was already absorbed in ideas for improvements, "up half the night or lying awake thinking about it, up before breakfast and forgetting to eat!" Beatrice, who had finally had the satisfaction of having a paper accepted by the *Journal of Chemical Physics,* felt she was learning an awful lot about the upper atmosphere and was helping Brian with some of the theory involved with his new ideas. She saw them as "a really good thing to start on next," meaning after they had reached Dallas.

They set off by air in October, having sent almost all their possessions ahead by ship. All our family was collected for a few days in Wellington. Our eldest daughter Rowena had just arrived with her sculptor husband, Jose Fajardo, and their small son from Venezuela, which was not a healthy place to be at that moment.

Jean and I had to tell ourselves, not for the first or last time, that we had brought our children to New Zealand to have a freer life, so who were we to complain if their excellent education there had given them the knowledge and self-confidence to work and flourish in wider spheres?

CHAPTER SIX

First Years in the U.S.A.

1963–1968

"We met Texas on the train, travelling all day through endless flat, square miles of dry grassland, scattered cattle and oil fields, and little old towns. A big, wide, fast highway followed the railway, and drivers were about the only human life we saw, apart from some local colour at breakfast in an old railway station, not unlike N.Z. facilities at their worst! However towards evening things changed a lot; the country got greener and prettier with trees and rivers, and we stopped a while at Fort Worth, which is an impressive city, very like Dallas in size. The suburbs run just about continuously to Dallas and we had a marvellous view of the skyline at sunset."

Beatrice was writing at the end of October from an apartment which they had found with the aid of a secretary from the Southwest Center. It was close to the Southern Methodist University (popularly known as S.M.U.) where the Center was actually located until its own buildings could be completed. The campus made an attractive setting, and included a cultural center containing a splendid small theatre and art gallery, presented by S.M.U.'s most famous alumnus, Bob Hope. Beatrice found the university atmosphere good, as was their welcome from friendly members of the staff. But she gained the impression from some of them that they "expected us to use an awful lot of money; e.g., an air-conditioned car is a must."

A day's shopping, however, convinced her that these people

43

were right about the car, and they would have to get one as soon as their travel money was refunded, "as life is geared to same to such an extent." For the time being, however, there was a cafeteria of the "eat all you can for a $1 type" down the road, and shopping in the supermarket was "great fun if you have time to investigate the many strange and varied packages of things on sale."

"In general we like the crowd at the Center greatly," she wrote a few days later. "Talk about international! In B's group they came from N.Z. (him only), Aussie, Canada, Ireland, all over the U.S.A., Norway and India—that's all I know at least. The Maths-Physics group includes N. Z., Hungary, Poland, Britain and (I think that's his place) Germany, and U.S.A. (one only). The leader of the group, Dr. Ivor Robinson, is evidently English, and is huge, gesticulating—with a plum in his mouth; extremely clever under all that and has been very helpful to me."

"One way and another we feel things are very promising here. The language is terrific! Texan differs greatly from San Franciscan, it's not easily understood and vice versa. However, any version of English goes at Southwest Center. No wonder they supply us all with Webster's dictionaries!"

A fortnight later they had bought a car and Brian had passed the stiff Texan driving test, though Beatrice hadn't yet dared to start driving. Brian had also heard from Dr. Ellyet in Christchurch that his Ph.D had been conferred, and Beatrice was managing to feel part of the group of mathematicians, even if not "participating in their work." "Next month," she wrote, "they are having an important international symposium on General Relativity and Cosmology (some exciting new ideas to be discussed). The people coming include Hoyle, Oppenheimer and just about every famous living man in the field from all over the world."

Naturally this was cause for great excitement but, before the symposium took place, Dallas had moved into the world news most unhappily. "Black date and black address" wrote Beatrice. "I feel ashamed to write it on the back." Not two miles from the Center Kennedy had been shot and "the whole city seems stunned—the people shocked and many weeping. Nearly everyone at the Center was pro-Kennedy and is genuinely really sad for the sake of America."

A month later she and Brian, sitting together at the Symposium, had "been inconspicuous and understood varying amounts of the papers and discussions. The atmosphere has been really thrilling as the extraordinary (in every literal and extreme sense) nature of newly discovered objects was revealed by the radio-astronomers from Australia and Joddrell Bank, and the optical astronomers from Mount Palomar and Lick, and as theorists from all over the world tried to think of mechanisms to account for them. Just to hear and see the varied interesting personalities of so many great scientists was marvellous. The pooling of ideas must have been of tremendous value to researchers, but I don't think they have any more certainty as to what the strange objects are than they did." She went on to describe at some length what she thought was the main problem, but concluded "I wish I knew enough to appreciate it fully."

The first two months in Dallas had certainly proved an exciting introduction to their new and much larger sphere of activity.

By Easter the following year, with the Center shut down for four days, she and Brian set out to explore the countryside taking "sleeping bags, primus and eats and books (relaxing type), and using the car as dormitory." After a night by some Texas lake, they crossed into Louisiana and drove as far as the Red River. "To get down to it, we left our car on a little road and trespassed—a bit scared as the fields belonged to very ugly old shacks with negroes in them, and we know that Lou. is one of those places where blacks and whites don't love each other. However, the lady we met was very friendly."

That night, back in Texas they "stopped where probably we shouldn't on a farm track just off a side road and had a ghastly experience. Everything had just stopped looking picturesque-at-sunset and spooky instead, and there was a big owl. Then a truck stopped on the road and we just stood and watched a man slowly load a huge gun, looking all round him, and shot the owl. Did we clear out of that haunted place as fast as our shivering limbs would let us!" Fortunately, fifty miles on they came to a State Park and, before settling in the car for the night, "ate canned grub off the primus in the most beautiful moonlit place imaginable. Woken in the morning by strange bird calls and a woodpecker tapping—It's been hard to get back to a relativity frame of mind."

A month later they drove to Washington, where Brian attended a conference while Beatrice went sightseeing. At the National Gallery, she was surprised at "how many of the world's great paintings are in America." They went together to the Senate and heard a Southern Democrat taking part in a filibuster against a Civil Rights Bill, "speaking to a nearly empty room—several times as many onlookers in the galleries." She thought his objections to the Bill were too trivial for anyone to be bothered with listening to them!

The drive home took three days, even though it was "hurried." "I loved driving through Virginia—picturesque countryside and lovely old farm houses" she wrote. "But parts of Mississippi and Alabama and Arkansas we saw were rather depressing. Beautiful country, but scattered with hovels housing negroes, compared with the prosperous great houses of the plantation owners, and sickening signs like 'Ladies—white' and 'Restaurant—for whites only' in a number of places. I see what people mean about hostility to foreigners—probably our voices are taken as northern. You can practically feel the hostility in the atmosphere."

All the same they arrived back in Dallas "spiritually refreshed by the trip," and a month later Brian's spectrometer had become a "visible thing" with several parts in his office. The mirror alone had cost $3,000, so he had good reason to be satisfied with his choice of the Southwest Center!

But Beatrice was not so happy, and by mid-July she was writing: "Big changes afoot in my life. In September I am enrolling in the Astronomy Department of the University of Texas in Austin for a Ph.D. The American system being unlike N.Z., I shall have to attend lectures and sit exams for two terms, then do a thesis. Austin being two hundred miles away this is rather a problem, but it is soluble and worth it. Here I seemed to have reached rather a dead end. Apart from the summer visitors, the line of interest among the Division was very much General Relativity as a mathematical game, with applications an incidental sideline if at all. And Ivor Robinson hasn't done much to enable me to follow things I'm interested in, which I suppose could be expected as he's so mathematical himself. So I have learned an awful lot of Relativity, but just don't get the right opportunities to use it to study astrophysics or physical cosmology. The only thing to do seems to be to take formal courses towards a degree in the right field, then do research for a thesis under helpful supervision—then be ready to produce something significant! Dallas doesn't seem to have any very scholarly universities (colleges), and nothing in my line anywhere, but the U of T in Austin has a well known Astronomy Dept. headed by an exceptionally brilliant (so everyone says—and he had an important contribution to the symposium last December) young man, and owning the 4th largest telescope in the world (MacDonald Observatory). So last week I went down and did a lot of talking and consulting and making lists, and arrangements are under way. I expect that I will fly down every Tuesday morning, and bus back (five hours but can read etc.) every Friday afternoon. I have rented a room in the home of a former professor's widow, which is nice and close. The considerable expense of all this, fares, fees and living (plus Brian eating out half the week!) can be met by my scholarship, which so far sits intact in our savings account. It took some deciding, to go back to lectures and exams, to travel four hundred miles a week (the people say it isn't far in Texas) and worst to be separated from Brian for four days and three nights every week. But we really think it will be worth it in the long run. I was getting depressed at my scientific stagnation, not having a baby either, and if my life is going to be science entirely it would be a waste to continue in the relativity group at the Center. A bit of separation for a couple of years ought to stimulate our relationship rather than spoil it! Anyway someone who feels they're achieving nothing isn't much to live with— I now have to start revising all the physics I knew in 1960 and 1961 for B.Sc and M.Sc exams, as well as learning some introductory astronomy, because in September I will be sitting a sort of test given by the Dept. to ascertain where the gaps in their graduate students' knowledge are! It would be a blot on the U. of Canty, not to mention me, if I couldn't at least choke up all the things I once knew. Luckily it isn't a matter of having to pass, but obviously I want to do just as well as possible."

She wrote again after her course in Austin had started: "Here we are back home for three and a half days till I go away for next week. Brian has driven 5,000 miles! seen a fabulous lot and decided to set up his brain child in Socorro, New Mexico. I've been working very hard at astronomy and am very glad of all the set-up down there; lovely room, thoroughly nice landlady, v.g. lectures, and the more astronomy I read the more interesting it gets. I qualified in their exam all right. Spent a very enjoyable evening with another N.Z. astronomy student and wife; he's about three years ahead of me on his way to Ph.D. and they're very poor students, because with their visa arrangements she can't earn money and he has a rather pitiful fellowship. I am the only woman student there and the others seem a nice sort of crowd. I was missing Brian horribly, though he sent about eight postcards and two long letters—Austin is very pretty and the Univ. atmosphere stimulating. I don't feel so cynical about Texas now."

I believe that Beatrice's cynicism at Dallas had been more due to the attitude of other wives at the Center than to sex discrimination on the part of men. For I recall her telling me that she caused consternation by refusing to 'pour,' when invited to take the teapot at some mixed gathering. This was turning down an 'honour.' Worse than that, she did so because she didn't want to be isolated from the men's scientific conversations, and apparently the wives didn't like the way the men included her on their sort of talk. As Brian's wife, rather than a scientist in her own right, she should have known her place and stayed in it!

When the Center moved into its own buildings in Richardson, their apartment in central Dallas became inconvenient. "Brian has to drive thirteen miles to work every day now," Beatrice wrote at the end of October, "and we are going to look for a nice place in North Dallas (which borders on Richardson) if possible.—I am working hard from Tuesday to Friday morning in Austin: 8 a.m. lectures on Wed. and Fri! I have a desk in a room full of other Astronomy Ph.D. students and study there or in the library along the passage and at my room in the evenings. It is a very pleasant walk to and fro. Work most interesting!"

One of her subjects for compulsory study was the American constitution and I recall her saying that it had taught her that the country really was a United States, with the states having far more differences from each other and more independent power than she had ever realised.

She and Brian quickly found a house to their taste and Beatrice wrote from Austin only three weeks later. "We have had a marvellous time the last two weekends getting us and some furniture into the house. The result is beautiful and we love living there already and can't imagine how we lived in a small flat with no view! B. had been complaining for months he never saw the sky. I haven't been getting claustrophobic since starting working here, but he is really enjoying the difference of a house and garden to live in. So am I!—Having acres of park out the back is lovely. You must come and stay with us."

When we did so eventually, we found that the surrounding

48

streets had no foot paths, though the nearest shop of any kind was almost a mile off, while the nearest bus stop was about four miles! It was indeed true, as Beatrice had been told on their arrival in Dallas, that a car was a must.

A month later she wrote: "I don't believe I have told you what my thesis is going to be about yet. Really I will be studying a whole lot of different theories of cosmology, to see which is best able to explain the observation made with optical and radio telescopes on different galaxies. The theories are based on Einstein's General Relativity (that means Steady State is excluded), and they represent different motions of the galaxies in the expansion of the universe, and different ages of the universe, different numbers of galaxies per unit volume of space, and so on. Using each theory one works out what to expect in observations of the faintest galaxies, quasars and radio sources. Then one tries to choose the theory that fits best. But I do not think the observations are complete enough yet for a real choice to be possible. The idea is to have a systematic and extensive set of calculations to compare with the observations as they become available, as it is a very interesting question which theory is best. An answer would have a lot of information about the past and future of the universe. The calculations also depend on what the various galaxies etc. were like at the time the light left them which now gets to the telescopes, and it isn't necessarily true that they were the same as nearby objects! So I will have to include a variety of different assumptions about the galaxies themselves, which will be a matter of astrophysics.

"Dr. Sachs suggests that a good systematic set of calculations is really needed, though lots of people have done bits of this before of course. He is very good at seeing things straight, and seeing the wood in the trees of calculations that have been done in the past; so I think I will have very good guidance from him. Already it looks a very interesting subject, because there are serious difficulties in trying to make any of the theories fit! (In case father remembers how fond people were of the Steady State idea several years ago, I should mention that there have been observations of radio sources which seem to have ruled it out entirely. Even Hoyle agrees.) Of course if it is impossible to explain the observations with any of the General Relativity theories, that will be worth finding out."—"P.S. Brian has just come home with a very pretty little cat which I've been persuaded to adopt."

Beatrice, Aged Three   *Primary School Girl*

"Mrs. Mop"   *High School Girl*

Debutante at New Plymouth

Bride of Brian Tinsley

Graduate at Canterbury

Professor at Yale

In mid-December Brian had his spectrometer out on the roof of the Center and life was "getting all unorganised. Last night I went out and left him there, then drove to the Ozvaths and played sonatas, came home and worked for several hours, slept for two, and went and fetched B. when he rang up at 4 a.m. He would have stayed till dawn but some cloud came up—The weather being clear he's off again tonight. Luckily I have plenty of things to do at home too! The astronomy work is going well and the weekly routine seems to be possible, leaving time for fun and energy to spare."

Over Christmas they took a break and went to Mexico City. Beatrice enthused over all the antiquities and thought the Museo de Anthropologia must be "about the most beautiful museum in the world. The central courtyard has a hugh monolith of the Aztec god of rain, about fifty feet high and five feet in diameter, supporting a roof hundreds of feet square and with a continuous shower of rain falling round the god." She didn't much enjoy a bull fight: "felt a bit sick. Quite an experience though and you can't say you've seen the things that make Mexicans tick if you haven't watched a bull-fight." The whole trip was necessarily short, as Beatrice had exams to pass in mid-January before she could start on her actual thesis. She, of course, passed them with no trouble!

By April Brian was "starting to get worried by the 'publish or perish' complex, having published nothing since he got here. I think he only imagines there is any such pressure, as so far he has had every sign of superior approval. (Anyway I resent the whole system of scientific prestige-building, but rebellion doesn't help.)" Brian was at work on a paper about the instrumentation aspects of his spectrometer and Beatrice could think of all sorts of ways for using it besides the examination of the geocorona for which it was built, and for which purpose Brian had been given a grant by the National Science Foundation.

She herself was "working on at the evolution of galaxies, for cosmological purposes and finding some quite interesting things." She stated that she had little idea how much was needed to make a Ph.D. dissertation but hoped to finish the degree in the next year or two, and "ultimately (i.e., when we are at the children-grown-up stage) look for a University teaching + research post—I feel very much that I would be a lot more satisfied doing teaching as well, not all research. On Saturday I am talking to a group of amateur astronomers (an annual convention) about quasars and cosmology—their request of subject. But I don't think they will know as much to start with as the very bright Junior Astronomers I talked to last month."

She was writing at the start of June and her reference to children at a grown-up stage was explained by their intention to adopt a baby, due to be born in New Zealand in August. In spite of much medical advice and even a small operation, after which the doctor had told her she was sure to conceive, there was no sign of Beatrice having a child of her own. But the idea of adopting one had only been focussed by learning of the advent of this particular child whose parentage they knew. Years later, when she and Brian had parted, Beatrice told me that she had hesitated considerably before agreeing to this adoption, because she was already suffering strains from their frequent partings while pursuing their separate studies, but not even when I have re-read the letters written at the time can I detect signs of an approaching marriage breakdown.

My wife Jean paid a brief visit to Dallas during that northern summer on her way home from visiting Rowena, who had returned to Italy from New Zealand. She was always very sensitive to atmosphere and on her return home she never mentioned signs of strain in Dallas. So, though I do not doubt that Beatrice later told me the truth, I believe that hindsight had magnified what had been at the time only a degree of uneasiness. And whatever her doubts were about the wisdom of adopting this child, I have no doubt that the boy himself brought her great happiness.

By June she was making preparation for his arrival and already possessed a beautiful folding crib and Dr. Spock's indispensable book, "which I study as a relaxation from galaxies." By mid-July the preparations were as complete as possible, while the prospective parents continued to work hard on their science. "Brian's new miniature spectrometer is completed and he tested it out in the lab last week and was very happy with the results. Next step is a test in a high altitude plane. I've been finding some very interesting results in my cosmology too, and believe the theory I've been working on since February may have some usefulness—to cosmologists and towards my degree!"

By August the eighteenth they were jumping every time the phone went, but, having cancelled their reservations for the following day, could not be in New Zealand till the 29th. Meanwhile Beatrice had gone to Austin and found Dr. Sachs "very pleased with all my results and the summary I left him a few weeks ago. It seems I've done enough research to get a Ph.D. with and now have only to write it all up, which I can hardly believe. That's only a few months work, even with a baby. Probably I could graduate at the end of the academic year, i.e., next May, though I hope the thesis will be written and oral exam over long before that. I was lucky to hit on a fruitful line of research and get some interesting results so soon. Of course it is still subject to the approval of the rest of my committee, including the Frenchman de Vaucouleurs who doesn't think anyone should get a Ph.D in less than five years whatever they've discovered. I'll have to sell it to him somehow—lots of references to his own work, perhaps!"

As it turned out the baby, Alan, put in his appearance on August 28th, so that their plane booking for the 29th was perfect. I recall them walking up the path to our home in Wellington with Beatrice carrying the baby and absolutely delighted. A certain amount of red tape had to be coped with and then they returned to Dallas, where their beautiful collie dog, Rata, immediately took to the baby. "She comes along and likes to lick his feet in a friendly way while he feeds." Soon Rata became so protective that she had to be restrained when visitors wanted to get near to see the baby!

Beatrice found that "public typists looked horrified at my thesis" and wanted at least a dollar a page. So, "what with that and the amount of time I would have spent visiting the typist and dressing Alan to take him along the best answer seemed to be to do it myself." So she hired an electric typewriter and using 'erasewell' paper "did it in less time than anyone else would have mainly because it meant something to me instead of being gibberish."

The "elegant machine," as she called it, was used for one of her letters to us. I don't know whether the paper was 'erasewell,' but there are no signs of erasures! Already the thesis was "DONE and is down town being duplicated. That will cost a fortune as there are 125 pages, 20 being graphs, and the only method of reproduction acceptable to the Graduate School is photo offset, which costs $3 a page. There are 50 copies for the same price as 1, so I will get 50 copies of the thing, costing $3 \times 125 = $375. The copies won't be wasted as people send out copies of their dissertations widely here, as pre-prints to everyone in the field. It will be another year before it appears in the journal. Hard to believe the final stages are here. The oral exam will be in the week before Christmas."

Actually it took place rather sooner, and by December 17th Beatrice had her Ph.D. She hadn't felt very proud of herself after the oral, "but they passed me."—"Afterwards I felt very anti-climatic and deflated, seeing no purpose ahead but washing and sweeping. But by now I am altogether happy at the thought of doing astrophysics in the spare time left by Alan and Brian, and being Alan's mother is my No. 1 priority as long as he is totally dependent all day. I might consider applying for a post-doctoral fellowship to do research at home for the next few months, and then spend a lot of it on getting daily help to do all the housework, so I can study while Alan is asleep and in the evenings, most of which Brian spends at the Center anyway."

This idea materialised in the following February, after they had been to New York for Brian to attend a conference at which Beatrice also gave a short paper. Alan went with them and was carried around various sights and art galleries. "It was funny" wrote Beatrice "changing Alan's disposable diapers under a twelfth century archway." This was at a place called The Castle, a real medieval castle which had been imported from Germany and rebuilt.

Back in Dallas Beatrice had found Thelma, "a lovely woman who works hard and cheerfully and is great friends with Alan." She came from nine to one-thirty five days a week, "earning money to pay lawyer's fees for adopting a one-year-old waif. So now I can divide my time between Alan, Brian and astronomy."

By 1967 all three of our daughters were out of New Zealand, one in the States and the other two in Italy. So Jean and I decided to visit them, and through a London agency we found a villa on the coast at Forte di Marmi near Florence, where the whole family could gather. Beatrice and Brian came over from Dallas and we had a memorable week by the sea, while an excellent Italian lady, whose services went with the villa, shopped and cleaned for us. Beatrice and Brian, with Alan, went on to Norway for a conference, and joined us again in London, where we had a flat in the home of Jean's sister, Beatrice's godmother Helen Hannay. After that we visited them in Dallas on our way back to New Zealand. So we saw a lot of them during that northern summer and it certainly appeared to be a very happy set-up.

But the small house in North Dallas was beginning to seem too small with a child, so it was no surprise when Beatrice wrote to say they had found a house in Richardson, "*just* what we want, on a *beautiful* section with lots of trees at the back." After some rather anxious negotiations it became theirs, and they took possession on New Year's Day 1968, less than two months later.

Meanwhile Beatrice had given a talk on T.V., which resulted in her "expounding cosmology to a high school science club." She didn't want "too many such invitations, as they involve many hours of preparation. But I always feel afterwards it's worthwhile if the kids are interested. Otherwise I'm reading, chasing Alan, violining, and chasing Alan. He climbs on the kitchen chairs now, so nothing is safe."

Brian was going away a lot to his observatory in New Mexico, but Beatrice said she was in no danger of getting bored. She was practising the violin in order to join the Richardson Orchestra, working with an organisation called Planned Parenthood, and "working on some problems in astronomy by mail with people and computer in Austin." Furthermore, and this may well have been the real reason for moving to a larger house, she and Brian were "applying to adopt a little girl from a Dallas adoption agency—I'm terribly excited about it."

Years later, when Beatrice told me of her hesitation about adopting Alan, I naturally asked her how she became so keen on adopting a second child. She admitted that this still puzzled her, but she thought it had been because she had not wanted Alan to be an 'only.'

A week before they were due to move house, Beatrice wrote: "I've been doing some very interesting cosmology in the last month, by mail and one trip to Austin, and much phone. Brian took a day of his vacation to stay home with Alan while I went to Austin. Brian has been given a salary raise and some very nice compliments for the New Year. That makes him very happy and will cover the difference in monthly payments on this house and the new."

For the house move they planned on "hiring Thelma (my ex-daily) and her husband and his truck for one or two days, which will be a lot pleasanter and hundreds of dollars cheaper than a moving company. More of Thelma's family turned up than expected. It rained all day but they enjoyed themselves. At lunch time we all ate bought fried chicken (a' la N.Z. fish'n chips) in the new house with a fire of newspapers in the grate, and I hope all parties in the house are as cheerful!"

Six days later they gave a large one for house-warming and Beatrice pronounced it "very successful. It was a terribly cold night (down to 10 degrees Fahrenheit before dawn) and everyone enjoyed the ugly crush, the fire and a huge jug of spiced wine. The next day freezing rain began and by Monday they even closed the schools because of a thin sheet of ice on all the roads. This happens once or twice a year in Dallas and nobody bothers with snow ploughs or chains (as they do up north when it lasts for months) and the city just stops moving."

Three weeks later Beatrice had done some productive work in cosmology lately via mail and phone calls to Deeming in Austin, and "I've given a couple of seminars on same to the relativity group at S.C.A.S. (they pay me $25 to prepare and spend 1–2 hours talking about observational cosmology with the four of them!, but the sitter takes several dollars of it)." She was also enjoying the Richardson Symphony Orchestra. "We're even tackling Brahms' first symphony. I fit in about an hour's practice a day."

By mid-February the adoption agency, called Hope Cottages, had "started interviewing us (1 together, 1 each separately and 1 home visit) for the baby and we have to have medical exams and the like. The interview I had was practically a psychoanalysis—very thorough and penetrating. We could have a little girl in as little as two months."

In early March her paper (incorporating thesis work) "at last" appeared in the *Astrophysical Journal*—"very prestigious, very slow, as I submitted it in June. What makes me happier still is that people have referred to my work and found it useful." Brian was home after two five-day trips and very pleased too that the flights with the spectrometer had been very successful. Alan was flourishing "running and playing around and loving life." As she wrote, he was outside getting muddy and playing with Rata. It was a picture of happy family life.

But she was becoming increasingly concerned with U.S. policies and the debacle in Vietnam. President Johnson, she stated, "seems to do nothing but proclaim the same, failed policies" and was almost ignoring the "very thorough and alarming commission report on the plight of the cities." Riots were inevitable in the coming summer. In fact they came sooner, breaking out soon after she wrote, and in her next letter she contrasted the billions of dollars spent on the Vietnam war with the "fraction of that amount which could have done so much to relieve the hopeless slum conditions." However, she was happy with the cosmology she was doing with a "prof in Austin. We hope our results will be published before too long." Also a student had been to lunch who asked her "to be on his Ph.D committee as he is following up my thesis work with some very interesting observation. It's good to keep a finger in the ink!"

The finger stayed there while she waited for news of the coming daughter, though it must have been hard to concentrate when Alan had become a real handful by himself, and she knew that news of the daughter plus the daughter herself could "come within a few hours of each other any day or six months from now."

The actual arrival came at a sad moment but for Beatrice truly providentially. For on May 7th my dear Jean, her much loved mother, died a few days after suffering a severe brain hemorrhage. Then three days later the new daughter was born.

Jean had left writings which showed most clearly that she had a premonition of her approaching death and was totally prepared for it. I told Beatrice of these and she wrote: "I have been feeling terribly sad for your sake, but if you feel and believe she died at the right time for her to die it must lessen the shock greatly. As you can imagine it hardly seems real here yet that Mummie isn't at home as always and I get waves of grief at odd moments of realisation or vivid memories."

But the shock of losing her mother was cushioned by other marvellous news. "On Tuesday we are bringing home our baby girl!—She will be eleven days old by then—was born on May 10th, the day of Mummie's funeral—Her name is Teresa Jean. We decided on it months ago and now wish we'd let Mummie know. Somehow this is perfect news for now. It is such a natural form of comfort that a new life begins in the family when an older person dies—I hope this letter makes you a lot happier."

CHAPTER SEVEN

Years of Domesticity

1968–1973

With two small children, plus a husband and house to care for, Beatrice necessarily became very domesticated. Baby Terry proved to start with exceptionally easy to look after because, as Beatrice wrote, "she's sleeping eight hours already, making up for it by stuffing in about eight little bottles between 7:30 a.m. and 11 p.m." Alan cooperated—he "was enchanted with the tiny thing" and didn't "seem to mind how much of my time Terry takes," finding "lots of important things to do in the garden." Even Rata, the collie, decided at once that the baby was part of the family and became "so protective that she practically has to be shut out of reach for a visitor to hold Teresa."

All this meant that Beatrice could fit in violin practice and continued to play some chamber music as well as taking part in the Richardson Orchestra. But there was no time for cosmology, even though she had every intention of returning to it eventually. In July she managed to spend an evening in the science library reading the latest science journals and rather sadly finding "how different the current problems will be by the time I'm active again."

She was the more tied to the house by Brian being so often away on his work. In mid-July, for example, he spent a weekend at his observatory in New Mexico and then, on the 26th, left for conferences in Spain and Norway, not returning till September 6th. Beatrice missed him "badly," as did Alan who "keeps losing and finding his photo in record cases and in his toy truck—a most pathetic game."

On the day of Brian's return there was a "nursery" crisis. He had left his suitcase half unpacked and Alan had got the aspirin bottle from the sponge bag! "I had to rush him to the doctor" wrote Beatrice, "and had his stomach pumped out. Five aspirins are fatal at his age and we had no idea how many he had taken from the bottle." Alan stood the ordeal well and actually ate a hearty breakfast on his return home. But his parents spent an unhappy day, with Brian "distraught," as signs of aspirin poisoning take eight hours to appear. But all was well in the end.

Perhaps because she was spending so much time at home Beatrice commented in her letters much more about local and world news, being equally incensed by the U.S. involvement in Vietnam and the Russian interference in Czechoslovakia. She was even more annoyed by a papal encyclical dealing with contraception. I had evidently criticised it in writing to her, but she went much further, writing: "I'm glad it is regarded as theologically unsound by many Catholics, so that lots of them won't take any notice (e.g. our friends the ——, who regard five as enough when they are nearing forty and want to put them all thru' university), but from my point of view I think his attitude is totally immoral anyway, as he admitted it will cause a lot of human suffering purely for doctrinal reasons! As to such idiotic conclusions that the use of contraceptions encouraged infidelity—surely even an old bachelor has enough insight (in his position) to realise the opposite is true!"

Her very strong feelings on this subject were soon to lead her to take action. Meanwhile she and Brian, when he was home, frequently took part in a small discussion group, closely resembling the Socratic Society at Canterbury University where they had first met, and spent long evenings delving into varied intellectual and social topics.

In October some Canterbury friends came to stay and they all went to the beach at Port Arkansas for three nights. "The others shared the responsibility generously, so I felt free to be alone a bit. (First break since we moved house and first swim since Italy). In the evenings the children slept like exhausted puppies."

At the end of the month the Richardson Orchestra held its last concert of the season and Brian "was surprised at how good we were!" He was having what Beatrice called a creative splurge, writing several papers. She, meanwhile, enjoyed playing quartets and fitted in a few hours each month at the library keeping up with astronomy. She still received occasional requests for the paper which had been published in February. The latest, which came from Czechoslovakia, made her realise "how long it is since I did any astrophysics! Time enough ahead—life is very full as it is."

Re-reading her letters I have realised that she had once more taken to signing herself quite often as "Beetle" rather than Beatrice or just B. This may have been, I feel, because spending so much time with her children took her back to her own childhood. But perhaps it was, too, due to the loss of her mother making her homesick and reminding her of the time when all our widely scattered family were together in New Zealand.

In January there came a more gentle reminder of the past when the Metcalfs, who had been spending a year in Boston, came to stay. The visit was "great fun," wrote Beatrice, "as they are among my very best friends" and they renewed old memories by once more playing chamber music together.

Shortly afterwards a "thirty seconds" appearance before a judge ended the trial period for Terry's adoption and, almost at the same time, Alan completed "all the formalities for his permanent U.S. visa, with a ridiculous medical exam and interview." What the interview was supposed to achieve Beatrice had no idea, but she told me later it almost seemed as though the U.S. was afraid of admitting a two-year-old communist!

The visa was needed because Brian was about to go to a conference in Prague and the whole family was flying to Europe with him so that Beatrice could visit her sister Rowena. They landed in Paris and drove to Italy through all the beauty of France in spring. Beatrice wrote from Florence that Jose was making beautiful sculpture but far too little of it, so that Rowena was really earning their bread and butter by translating business letters. This kept her busy much of the time Beatrice was there, but she felt she had really got to know her sister again and, when Brian arrived from Prague, the two couples enjoyed evenings out together at a concert and a discotheque.

Back in what Brian called the "land of modern buildings, big cars, air-conditioning and T.V." they found that the Southwest Center was about to become the University of Texas at Dallas. This meant that it would be a "campus of U.T. authorised at present to take third year students." Beatrice approved of the change, having always felt that the "S.C.A.S. has rather a sterile air, being full of research scientists and no students." She did not think it would make any difference to Brian, as his research was funded by the U.S. Government.

Before the change in the Center's status actually took place Beatrice was given what she called a fictitious appointment as a visiting scientist. This was done at the suggestion of the head of Brian's section of S.C.A.S., and it paid for "some computing and making pre-print copies" of a short paper on cosmology she had managed to find time to write. In early June it was "sent hopefully off to a journal."

However, when Brian departed to a further conference in Spain where he was to read a paper, Beatrice started a very different activity, "collecting old clothes from S.C.A.S. wives as a Wives Club contribution to the poor Indian community in Dallas." I recall her telling me that she thought the Indians were worse off than the black people, and in a letter written after she collected the clothes explains her concern. "They arrive from the country looking for better opportunities in the city (this happens everywhere), and first of all don't have suitable clothes, which makes looking for a job even harder, and of course don't have any money to buy any. Also they have usually vast families, but unfortunately I couldn't do anything to help in that respect this time! I drove down with the car so full there was hardly room for Alan and Terry, and unloaded all the boxes into a Mission School building, reminiscent of a N.Z. rural Sunday School. It was pretty obvious from the surrounding houses that the people are *poor,* and also that the city keeps their streets in a ghastly condition compared to the wealthier areas."

For a long while both Beatrice and Brian had been urging me to visit them, and I took the chance to do so, in October on my way to Britain to celebrate my mother's eighty-fifth birthday. It, however, was not an entirely happy visit. I found Beatrice very strung up, as well as extremely intolerant of diverse opinions. I was no doubt foolish to be drawn into arguments about Christianity and abortion, about which in advance I really knew we could not agree, but I was abashed to find (as I wrote to Theodora), that Beatrice seemed to regard me as a 'nitwit' and that I found Brian much more tolerant of divergent views. I also expressed concern at the way she shouted at the children, though I had to admit that they seemed happy.

One evening there was party when the conversation was fascinating, but all their scientist friends appeared to be atheist or agnostic and I felt isolated. Next day, however, Beatrice drove me the two hundred miles to Austin, where we stayed with Dr. Harlan Smith, the head of the astronomy department. Beatrice, who had a paper to deliver next day, went to bed early with a cold, and I discovered that both my distinguished scientist host and his wife were Christian believers and had shown their commitment to the Lord by adopting four Korean orphans. I think I must have been mellowed by a long talk with them when, so he said, we seemed like old friends. For, when we drove back through the following night to Dallas, I felt myself much closer to Beatrice. So the visit ended happily.

Looking back I believe the tremendous tension I could not but sense was due in large measure to the clash between her devotion to science and her equal or greater devotion to her children, husband and home. When she adopted Alan and Terry she had seen clearly that some years away from astronomy would be inevitable. But simply seeing the problem was not solving it, and the clash between the two strongest forces in her personality had made her a very frustrated young woman.

Her state of tension, however, was not apparent in her letters, which continued as affectionate and frequent as ever. A month after our drive to Austin, I was in Florence staying with Rowena, and Beatrice wrote about a new development in her life, consequent on the change of status at the S.C.A.S. "I've started giving lectures to Brian's astronomy students on Tuesday and Thursday afternoons, which is a pleasant change. There are four students in the room and three more on closed circuit television, which is disconcerting—It's amusing to see myself on the monitor in front of me."

Behind their home there were always blue-jays and squirrels in the trees, and just before Christmas that year there was a special visitor, a red cardinal bird, which took up residence in the garden. "What is amusing," wrote Beatrice, "is that he spends hours a day pecking on the bedroom window, where he apparently takes his image for an intruder on the property. As long as he doesn't break his beak or the window the company is lovely."

In the new year she applied for a part-time job teaching maths at a local college. She was not too upset when she heard nothing, she wrote, and later definitely glad not to have been given the job. For the college had been virtually blacklisted by the Association of University Professors for its low standards and lack of academic freedom. In spite of that, however, the shortage of jobs was such that they had received 78 applications for a low-paid post teaching physics from highly qualified people.

This underlined how greatly Brian was valued both by the university and the National Science Foundation, which was paying for him to go to a conference in Leningrad in May. He and a friend stayed there for two and a half weeks, which were valuable, but then left early because there was nothing further to interest them and they found it impossible to visit even advertised beauty spots because of the inefficiency or laziness of Intourist. Even leaving the country was not easy. At the frontier with Finland they had papers they really valued, and which had already been published, confiscated by the Russian customs because they had not been stamped for export!

Shortly afterwards Beatrice and Brian joined the Richardson Unitarian Church, which she described as a "very congenial community, that being the only sense in which it is a church." "The Minister is a liberal intellectual—like most of the congregation he's an atheist." Some years later I attended this so-called church and was puzzled when the congregation recited a creed which included the words "our prayer is work." I could not understand what a congregation of agnostics and atheists meant by prayer. But there is no doubt that Beatrice and Brian found inspiration from the Minister whom Beatrice described as an "excellent speaker, who reads vast numbers of books and gives sermons that are really worth listening to."

Soon after joining the church Beatrice became secretary to the first Dallas branch of a national organization called Zero Population Growth, ZPG for short. It absorbed much of her time and energy, especially because she was responsible for producing and circulating a newsletter. The August copy ran to five hundred copies of five pages each, produced on a gestetner and sent by post! She commented "Don't mind working for an essential cause." Not long afterwards the branch held a public meeting, which was a great success. "Even a T.V. reporter (whose husband was a Texas congressman) came and gave us a beautiful report next night. The head of the Dallas County child adoption unit also came and joined up. The unit now has a white person wanting to adopt a negro child." This was against the state law in Texas, and Beatrice was hoping that this specific case would be an open challenge to such an outdated and racist enactment.

She was still busy with ZPG when Brian went to Brazil that autumn to look for a new site for his spectrometer, but she was able to find some time for research in astronomy. Alan was attending a Montessori school, and Beatrice discovered that the staff there would also welcome little Terry in the mornings. "It's wonderful to have all that time to myself," she wrote. "Then I do the house-work after lunch when A and T are home. Very happy. Terry is also very happy at school, though I haven't much idea what she does. Montessori likes to take them at 2. It's a big expense (will be $435 for Terry by the end of the year in May), which we regard as the cost of me doing astronomy rather than making any vital difference to Terry. If I do some successful research in the next month or two I might get a post-doctoral salary of some kind for next academic year. Meanwhile inflation plus two school fees have taken up the gain in B's salary. Not that we live badly now! Brian was lucky (not meaning undeserving) to get a raise at all at a time when lots of physicists are losing their jobs or taking pay cuts."

Brian was in Brazil for two months, arriving home on December 12th, only just in time for Beatrice to do his washing and ironing before she flew to Austin for a conference on Relativistic Astrophysics. She wrote from there: "I just finished in time the paper I've written with an astronomer in Berkeley and have brought some pre-print copies to distribute to people interested in the work." Writing from home a week later she told of "lots of useful conversations with people whose names are familiar from their research papers. Also, which is important to me in my relative isolation from astronomers, a number of people were very generous with pre-publication copies of exciting new data."

So the year ended with Beatrice once more involved in astronomical research far sooner than she had expected when she adopted the children though she was still, of course, tied down almost entirely to working at home.

The next year deepened her re-involvement. On January 16th she wrote "I've spent a lot of time in the last two weeks writing research proposals to funding agencies. The Univ. of Texas in Dallas at present calls me a visiting scientist and provides an account to pay for my computing, publishing etc costs. But they have now formally decided the conditions under which they will pay a salary to the spouse of a faculty member. It means that to get the part-time research job I want, I have to obtain my own funds independently of any member of the institution. Elaborate way of avoiding favoritism! Rather a tough assignment too for someone as un-heard-of as me. But I'm trying to get the necessary funds from the National Science Foundation, which funds nearly all astronomy in the country. Luckily NSF programme director in the field is a friend of mine from a number of past meetings, so he might be sympathetic."

By March Brian already knew that he would be financed to go to a further conference in Russia, this time in Moscow, while Beatrice was planning to attend a three-day meeting of the American Astronomical Society in Baton Rouge at the end of the month. Just before she went Brian wrote to tell me that she had been given a grant of $500 from the Sigma Delta Epsilon fraternity, but she might well have a long wait for the $20,000 which she had asked for from the National Science Foundation, as funds for scientific research "are in very short supply nowadays."

Beatrice was continuing with her ZPG work and on April 22nd, which was called Earth Day, she was due to talk on population control to a high school in the morning, which scared her more than talking to astronomers. Two months later she wrote: "My evenings are so full of things like ZPG business that it's hard to fit in *any* astronomy without those mornings," that was to say mornings when the children, who had just been having a holiday, had gone back to school. However, she increased her work for Zero Population Growth, becoming a trustee and secretary-treasurer to "Oasis," which was described as "a trust organisation that makes referrals for sterilisation operations, (which are legal locally but hard to find a doctor) and abortions (for which they have to go to New York or New Mexico)." Her life was certainly full but, so she stated, "a lot calmer now that Terry passed the magic third birthday."

Beatrice had planned a further visit to Europe to see Rowena again, but this plan fell through when Brian went on a specially chartered plane. Instead she and Brian had a splendid holiday in the Rockies before he went and, on her return to Dallas, she wrote to say that she had obtained her "grant of funds from the National Science Foundation and will be a paid scientist as of next Monday." The grant was for part-time work, and when exactly she did it "nobody will know or care, as long as my output is satisfactory." She was particularly glad that it had arrived in time to pay for travel and living expenses for a meeting at Amherst after Brian's return from Moscow.

At Amherst she was impressed when a "*very* eminent woman astronomer—great enough to win any honors in any contest—turned down a prestigious prize offered to women astronomers (only) on the ground that special honors and discrimination for women should be abolished. It caused a gasp and then applause from the assembled throng, but the chairman—a delightful charismatic Dutchman—cut off all comment by setting up a special committee to study the matter and 'inviting polite letters from those with well considered opinions.' It certainly woke up some of those there as to what problems (not all discriminatory of course) women face and how deeply they are felt! I've written (I hope politely) to the committee."

By the end of September she was planning a further step towards returning to full time science. "I'm probably going to spend Jan–March next year at Pasadena, California," she wrote, "where I have been invited to work with some astronomers at the Hale Observatories (the 200 inch Palomar telescope), doing theoretical work, not observing of course. If all goes as planned, I'll take the children and have them in school all day. Brian hopes to spend most of that time in Brazil and/or at the McDonald observatory in West Texas. In spite of the nuisance of upheaval (and probably letting the house) it's a fantastically interesting and exciting offer and impossible to refuse. It's just a three month visiting appointment for which I'll have to get leave of absence from U.T. Dallas. It should be confirmed next week."

As it turned out Brian went to West Texas for a week in early November to set up a new spectrometer, and immediately afterwards flew off to Brazil, stopping en route to find a site in Peru at which to locate the spectrometer in 1972. His return was delayed till Christmas Eve, and only a few days later the whole family set off for California by car.

Beatrice's first letter from Pasadena was concerned mostly with having found an old but convenient house and a good Montessori school for the children where they could stay from 8:15 in the morning till 5 p.m. when she left work. They had been up to the Mt. Wilson observatory but had only seen the 100-inch telescope from the visitor's window as no faculty member was there to let them in. Terry had been sick in Los Angeles and they had thought it was due to the notorious smog. But it turned out to be caused by nervousness about going to a new school where, however, she had settled in at once.

Beatrice too settled in quickly. "I'm working very hard," she wrote, "enormously enjoying life being surrounded by eminent astronomers and astrophysicists. This is a very prestigious place, of course, due to the 100 inch and 200 inch telescopes. Lunch times are very fruitful. The astronomy dept. has a big table at the faculty club, where the food is excellent and inexpensive, but overlooked in the conversations. I'll be going back to Dallas with enough ideas to last for years, not to mention many good new friends."

The next letter, a fortnight later, was on impressive notepaper headed "Mount Wilson and Palomar Observatories." Beatrice explained that, while Mt. Palomar was farther off and she had not been there, "Mt. Wilson is very close by, being up the mountains behind L.A. and in a very clear spot just above the inversion layer—i.e., all the smog stays below."

By the end of February she had been north to "Santa Cruz (where the astronomy dept. runs the Lick Observatory) talking with many people and giving a couple of colloquia on my work. Came back with millions of new ideas to follow up, and wishing I could spend more time with some of those people." She described the Santa Cruz campus as consisting "of scattered buildings hidden in trees on a vast acreage of farmland, reminiscent of Taranaki in vegetation and coastline—idyllic place." A few days later, when Brian had come to stay, they went to a beach "where there was a thick fog which hid the people more than fifty yards away and hid the highway, so we enjoyed the sea and the rock pools and sand a lot. Coming home it was sunny and clear on the mountain top, but sultry and smoggy down the other side in Pasadena. I must say I relished the fresh air up in Northern California."

With Brian back in Brazil at the end of March, Beatrice had the chance to stay with the Gunn family in the guest cottage on Mt. Palomar, where James was doing a week of observations. "I lost much sleep," she wrote, "as I spent half of Friday night observing observers at the various telescopes, but then had to rise with Alan and Terry to get them *quietly* fed and out of the house to let the Gunns sleep till noon." "Saturday I went to bed very early after a most exciting hour watching the 200 inch telescope and its electronic paraphanalia in action. I'd love to learn to observe when the kids are older." "The vast scale of the 200 inch and its dome is terribly impressive. The huge thing is so beautifully mounted that it runs on a tiny 150 horsepower motor."

By the beginning of April she and Brian were both back in Dallas, but Beatrice left for the West Coast almost at once for an Astronomical Society meeting in Seattle. She enjoyed it as much as anything because she had already made friends with so many of the astronomers there. Meeting them again was an inspiration, and two months later, though missing the stimulus of Caltech, she was still happily working on ideas she had gained there.

At the same time she was hoping to be promoted to an assistant professorship at U.T.D. instead of being a mere visiting scientist. She explained that the authorities were likely to get into trouble if they don't upgrade the status of women. "Currently one faculty member out of fifty-two is a woman!" Sad to say her hopes for such a promotion in Dallas remained unfulfilled, even though she designed the Astronomy Department there in which, by a strange irony, Brian was later to become a lecturer.

The whole family went to California for their summer holiday and Beatrice stayed on to give a "well received paper" at a "very profitable" conference in San Francisco. Back home she was still involved in ZPG and was surprised one day to find herself on a radio programme, when she had not realised that the answers she had given on the phone had been taped for broadcasting!

In the fall my wife Mattie and I went to stay with them. I had remarried at the start of 1971, and we had spent the summer of 1972 sight-seeing in Europe and meeting relatives and friends in Britain. We found Beatrice so totally organised that it was virtually impossible to help with the household chores to which we inevitably added. But we greatly enjoyed our stay both in her home and on outings with children. These included a visit to the State Fair, where one gained a much better impression of the traditional Texas than was possible in the urbanised 'yankeeness' of Dallas. The garden at Laguna Drive, with its birds and squirrels, not to mention toads which came out of the grass to eat the dog's leftovers, was a haven from the endless road signs and rushing traffic in the town and a splendid playground for the children.

As soon as we left Beatrice flew once more to Pasadena for a conference where she gave two papers. They were both "well received," she wrote. "I feel specially gratified about my own one as I think it was on the best work I've done and a significant discovery—others think so too. The paper about Hoyle's theory was also accepted by all but Fred, though nobody took his line of defence seriously. I had a very good conversation with him about it, and we basically agreed that Barnothy and I showed very serious difficulties for his theory though not insuperable ones. Also made some progress in my collaboration with Jim Gunn, who has already put in many nights observing at the 200 inch telescope on our joint project. (It's exciting having that big eye turning out data specially for me!) I'm going over for two weeks in February for a solid attack on the project."

Winter came early to Dallas that year. Brian, who had spent a week of beautiful days at the McDonald observatory, returned to a gale that stripped the trees and was followed by an unusual November snowfall. Then, on December 13th, Beatrice wrote "We've just had a fantastic ice storm. It hailed three inches on Sunday night and remained at about 25 degrees, then rained a little, which froze to a perfect glaze. The roads were ghastly—couldn't even walk outside, and the trees looked like a dreamland of heavy long icicles. All the schools closed down and most businesses"—"I've seen hail and icy roads in Texas before, but this was incredible. Exciting, but I didn't need the time off work between now and our departure." The "departure" was for a three-week visit to New Zealand, where we were delighted to entertain them all for a few days in our Wellington home.

Back in Dallas, Beatrice worked "very hard" on her "proposal for an Astronomy Dept. at U.T.D." "It looks hopeful," she wrote, "fairly sure to get approval here, but the State Coordinating Board may not want it. The proposal has to be written in the most nauseating jargon. I read three other proposals through, drank a glass of wine, then translated my straightforward English into a fairly good imitation."

But, while still hoping for upgrading to a more permanent position at U.T.D., she accepted a temporary lectureship at the University of Maryland. The fortnight at Caltech was reduced to a "fruitful" week, and then the whole family set off by car once again, this time for College Park, near Washington, where the University of Maryland is located.

CHAPTER EIGHT

Separation

1973–1974

The drive to Maryland was an endurance test, taking three days on two of which the car broke down. Terry was again sick from apprehension, but both children adapted quickly to yet another school.

Beatrice found in nearby Silver Springs "a nice roomy house belonging to a University of Maryland professor on sabbatical. Also very expensive, but all real estate is tremendous here." Brian left for Peru, and she settled to "an interesting course to teach and much research to do, mostly now on projects from Cal:tech, but more coming here." She ended the letter "Missing Brian."

A month later she apologised for not having written for so long but "My writing energies have gone into several papers with deadlines—(Usually defined as the date on which the editor drops dead if he's got the manuscript! Mine was in no danger) Also it's been a hectic two weeks. Last week there were visits to Maryland from a woman astrophysicist I knew at Cal:Tech, and she needed a lot of driving round (which I was glad to do—great friend) and we spent time together. Then from a man at Princeton with whom I share my research interests, and that took time off my own rush jobs. I got through the week somehow!, including a busy one day trip to New Haven, Connecticut, where I was invited to talk at Yale and spend hours with my collaborator on some fascinating problems on galaxy formation. That was a very enjoyable trip as several Yale astronomers are old friends. By Saturday I was ready to spend the week-end with the children and get everything ready for my Sunday departure for a two day conference in Austin. (Very nice and competent university student came to stay with A and T, as she did all day when I went to Yale). However at 8:30 a.m. on Saturday Brian called from Miami to say he was on his way to Washington! Back two weeks early, because his equipment was still en route from Brazil. So we spent Saturday and half Sunday all here together. The children were delighted at the surprise (so was I!) and we had a great time. Then B and I flew to Dallas together on Sunday, and I got up very early on Monday to get to Austin as I was the second speaker at the conference.

"Spring is coming here—blossoms and daffodils everywhere. We all had a gorgeous walk on Sunday in the vast regional park, noticing how many trees were in bud since two weeks ago."

The letter ends, not surprisingly, "No chance of stagnating!" It was only fifteen months since Beatrice had found it a tough assignment to get research funds, because she was so "unheard of." But during that time she had clearly made her mark among astronomers and cosmologists of many universities throughout the United States. She and Brian had both come a long way since they arrived rather shyly on the campus of the Southern Methodist University ten years earlier to join S.C.A.S. Beatrice was well aware of this. When she told us that inflation and rising prices meant that her lectureship in Maryland had not been "a profitable job financially," she added: "Luckily it's been (and is) a great boost professionally. I find myself now an accepted member of the community of cosmologists and astrophysicists—gratifying fulfillment of long dreams! The work is a great pleasure to me."

By then Brian's spectrometer had finally reached Peru. It had been there once on a train, but had accidentally been returned to Brazil! This time it came by ship round the Horn and had been duly installed on a sixteen thousand foot mountain at Huancayo. So, after arranging for assistants to operate it, Brian returned to the U.S. and came to live for a short while in Silver Springs. He had been given a grant to work for two months at the Naval Research Laboratory in Washington and the Goddard Space Flight Center nearby, both close enough to Silver Springs for commuting to work.

At the end of August they returned to Dallas together in

time for Beatrice to leave for Europe, where she planned once more to visit Rowena in Florence before going on to a conference in Poland. The visit to Rowena was a success, but unfortunately there was a case of cholera in Italy, and the Poles demanded an inoculation six days old before admitting travellers who had been staying there. Beatrice reached Vienna without knowing this. A postcard from the airport stated "I got one, but the I.A.U. will be over in six days. Going straight to my friends in Paris. Very disappointed."

So, after spending a long day at Vienna Airport on a waiting list for flights, she finally reached Paris at 9 p.m., "in a muddle about what country and what language I was in!" But she was happily received by her friends the Audouzes in their beautiful large flat. Jean, whom she had anyhow meant to consult after the Warsaw conference, set off for Poland next morning. But Beatrice and Madame Audouze, who was a distinguished archaeologist, enjoyed each other's company, and Beatrice did a lot of sight-seeing "perhaps getting as much as I would from papers on cosmology." When Jean returned she met many astronomers who had just been names before—with some surprises! "There are a lot of women and they sign their names with initials only, so people I'd imagined to be men even had the wrong sex. On the last day I had a formal colloquium, which generated a lot of interesting questions (the most satisfying response) and an invitation to dinner with an eminent couple of astronomers who live in a pent-house apartment above another part of Paris."

On returning home she found that the children had been so happy where they were billeted that she was contented to let them go to the same people for half of each week, while she travelled to Austin to teach and work with astronomers there. Brian had been to a conference in Japan and stopped in Alaska on his way back to set up a spectrometer on a roof in Fairbanks to do what he called "auroral observing."

Beatrice came back from Austin each weekend, and as she had found a maid to come in and clean the house, she was free to spend much more time with the children. One weekend she took them camping with a group from the Unitarian Church, and as they all sat out late round a "vast bonfire—the stars were very inspiring—Terry asked if there were infinity of them. Maybe that's something I'll help find out in the next few years."

At the time the Watergate scandal was coming to light and

Beatrice found she could "give no credence whatever to Nixon." "This doesn't mean," she wrote, "that I don't think the American system of Government is potentially as good as any. But the checks and balances are all out of equilibrium, with so much money involved in political campaigns, so much lobbying power in enormous financial entities, and so much unchecked power in the executive branch. In the light of all the recent disclosures, the last presidential election made a sheer farce out of democracy."

The year finished as busily as it had begun. In the first week of December, Beatrice went to Tuscon, Arizona, for an astronomy meeting, then almost immediately to Austin for the last week of classes, followed by the final exams. "I had to get them graded for a crazy deadline," she wrote, "so spent Saturday night plus Sunday plus Sunday night going over a hundred and thirty three hour papers! Now home till after Christmas." That was true, but even before New Year she left again for a week at Caltech "squeezing in some hard work on my continuing research with Jim Gunn out there before classes start again."

She really enjoyed her week at Caltech, not just because of progress on the big project with James Gunn about the evolution of galaxies, but because it was a great satisfaction "to go back there among all those famous astronomers and be greeted like and treated as a respected colleague." By the end of the month this status was confirmed by an invitation to spend three weeks in July and August ("all fares paid") at the Institute of Theoretical Astronomy in Cambridge, England. "I'll probably be giving a lecture or two," she wrote, "and learning a lot from others, and getting a lot of research done with people from all over the world who gather in Cambridge for summer."

She continued going regularly to Austin, though finding it a "rather harrowing place" because of disagreements in the Astronomy Faculty between the conservative elder members and the younger ones like herself about the future curriculum. She noted that Dr. Harlan Smith, the head of the department whom I had liked so much, was "on the right side." I never heard the outcome of the disputes, though Beatrice continued to teach at Austin for the rest of the year.

Her summer programme was further filled up by an invitation to give a series of lectures to a selected group of international students at a summer school during May at Erice in Sicily, and before going there she gave talks at Chicago, Urbana (Illinois) and Bloomington (Indiana). "Erice," she wrote, "is a fascinating and beautiful little town. Funny to be mixing the latest astronomy with ancient ruins and walking about on elaborately cobbled streets.—I haven't learnt much astronomy though I hope I've taught some, and what I have learnt was at breakfast with the other teachers.—-The students were mostly at a rather disappointing level, but so mixed that if you said things geared to the worst the best (who are practising astronomers in the field) would be bored." However, the social side of the gathering was splendid, and she made new friends among international astronomers.

She arrived back in Richardson just in time for Brian to leave for Paris and Brazil. Then the whole family joined Rowena and her children at Huancayo. Not unexpectedly Rowena had finally decided to leave her charming but improvident husband, and Beatrice, who had talked with her briefly at Rome airport while returning from Erice, was sure she was wise to decide to make a new life on another continent.

Before she herself left for Peru she heard that she had gained the Annie Cannon Prize in Astronomy, "a great surprise to me since the change in the terms of the award means that this year it was an open competition for the first time among all female astronomers in the U.S. under 35 (it used to be for senior women astronomers)." The award was for $1,000, "not to be sneezed at," although it wouldn't go far in paying for publication of papers. Beatrice planned to use it to pay for travel involved in her researches into the evolution of elliptical galaxies. She sent us a copy of the very lucid statement of her intentions which had accompanied her application for the prize, and one can well understand how the clarity of her thinking and ability to express herself would have impressed the judges. She was just thirty-two at the time she won the award in open competition. So, even if it was for women astronomers only, gaining it was a real honour.

Then Mattie and I received an unpleasant surprise, when she let us know, just before leaving for Huancayo, that she and Brian had started divorce proceedings. Apparently these could continue under the state law of Texas, even though they were going to be together for some while! She had delayed telling me, she stated, because she knew I would be upset, as indeed I was, perhaps more than I would have been had we been warned. For, as has appeared in what I have quoted, Beatrice had often repeated that she missed Brian when he was away, and recalled, even when she told us a final break-up was forthcoming, that they had many good times together.

I do not propose to record all the reasons she gave then and later for the divorce, but undoubtedly conflict between their careers was a contributing factor. Trying to go on working at U.T.D., she wrote, "had reduced me to a state of mental anguish. Hard to explain! I am a good scientist, and among my peers treated like a full and respectable person and feel of *worth*. U.T.D. has kept me at the nearest possible level to nothing and there is *no one* who knows enough about astronomy to care in the least for my work. Austin has helped, but it is a second rate job (underpaid, half-time) at a department much worse than I'm worth. This isn't supposed to be boasting. To be rejected and undervalued intellectually is a *gut* problem to me, and I've lived with it most of the time we've been here, apart from extended visits to Cal:Tech and Maryland and shorter trips and meetings and so on."

Brian's work had been, of course, and still was, very highly valued at U.T.D., which had given him the chance to build the instruments he invented and to use them as far afield as Brazil and Alaska. It had been shown too that important government agencies valued his work highly. It was, in fact, virtually impossible for him to think of moving. So there was a very deep conflict between their vital interests, when Beatrice could find no work worthy of her talents in the same place.

And, if it was not clear to the authorities at U.T.D. that she was an important cosmologist, it was soon demonstrated that she was so in the opinion of others. Before leaving Cambridge she had been asked to go and work there for three years, and on her return home, while she continued with her part-time job in Austin, she was deluged with invitations to lecture at other universities. Cornell in Ithaca (New York) was followed by Chicago and Yale; then five days at the Kitt Peak National Observatory in Tuscon (Arizona), and when she spoke to the staff of the Bell Labs in New Jersey she was offered a job "as a sort of astronomer consultant to their high-powered experimental physicists. I couldn't have stood the company atmosphere," she commented, "compared to a university."

Shortly afterwards both Chicago and Yale universities offered her Assistant Professorships, with a distinct possibility of Cornell also making an offer if an expected vacancy occurred in the staff. As between Yale and Chicago, she thought the latter "the better place as a scientific institution," but Yale had "a very congenial small select group of astronomers, whom I would like to join" and was in a "small highly cultured New England town." Chicago wanted an answer by the end of October, and it must have been during the few weeks preceding the deadline that she attended a party at U.T.D. In what had presumably been a last effort to save her marriage she had applied to be made head of the Astronomy Department she had designed. There had been no reply and at the party the man who should have answered remarked casually, "I have a letter from you, don't I, that I must answer some time." She told me later that she took a somewhat vicious pleasure in replying "You needn't bother now. I'm choosing between Chicago and Yale!"

She was, in fact, already thinking she would "choose Yale for its civilisation," having a vague feeling "it would be selling my soul to go to Chicago." Also she already had at Yale "a valued collaborator, and I would take his word for its being a delightful place to live and work." Before she could go to Yale, however, she was committed to spending six months at Santa Cruz on the campus which had so greatly attracted her two and a half years earlier.

Meanwhile she was concerned that the children should be as prepared as well as possible for her departure, as they were to stay behind in Dallas. She had agreed to their staying with Brian, who became their legal parent. "I have no doubt," she wrote, "that it is better for them to stay with him in the place they have always known, with their friends, school, child minders etc, rather than to trek around the place with me. Also, I have no doubt Brian is an excellent parent." She became the "possessory conservator!" which meant "sending money, having visits, etc." She hoped that the fact that so many of their young friends had separated parents would make it easier for the children, but she herself found the preparation to leave by no means easy. She had moved into a flat of her own on returning from Huancayo, but spent a good deal of time with them, even moving back into Laguna Drive for a week when Brian was in South America. She wanted to ensure that the children continued to love both their parents, and it was because she meant to see as much of them as possible, that she had turned down the highly prestigious offer of three years at Cambridge. It was "too far away," so she had consented only to return for the next summer school.

Less than a fortnight before leaving for California she wrote: "I'm enjoying four days with Alan and Terry. They are so full of energy and love. It hurts. But I can tell they are O.K., and lots of people love them."

Years later, during our last long conversation on a hill overlooking New Haven, Beatrice wondered whether the intense trauma she suffered in leaving the children had triggered her melanoma cancer, which had been lying dormant. It is clearly impossible to say whether that was true, but that she even thought it might be showed me that she did not reveal the full extent of her suffering at the time.

She planned to leave on Christmas Day after attending a gathering of astronomers in Dallas at which she and James Gunn spoke of the tentative conclusions from their research. She sent us a copy of the report on their speeches, which appeared in the *New York Times*.

Then came the actual departure, when she "left Brian and Alan and Terry opening their Xmas presents. (At least the children had lots of new toys to cushion the realisation that I was leaving.)" After that she drove to Pasadena with a friend.

CHAPTER NINE

Interlude in California

1975

The two-thousand-mile drive to California proved to be something of an ordeal. The friend was in such a state of depression as to be "nearly irrational," so Beatrice did not dare to let her share the driving. But, having delivered her in Pasadena, she spent three days "catching up on Cal Tech friends and their astronomy, which was marvellous." Then on up the "gorgeous coast road" to Santa Cruz, "nine hours of slow bends and perfect views. Car was o.k.—just got a flat yesterday in the Lick parking lot." The actual Lick observatory, she explained, was up on Mt. Hamilton, but a building on the campus was known as the Lick Observatory and that would be her best address, although she had already found an apartment down the hill from the university buildings. It was, she wrote "a gorgeous place," "upstairs, looking down a hill of fields along a line of big gum trees, out to sea. I'm paying a lot of rent for the view, but after all those years in the middle of Texas it seemed worth having the sea to gaze at. Further up the hill is the U.C.S.C. campus, which is lost in a beautiful redwood forest. I look out of my office window into the forest. It is lovely to have such beautiful surroundings!"

A few days later she sent us further newspaper reports of the talks which she and James Gunn had given at the Dallas conference. The *Los Angeles Times* reporter had taken the trouble to talk to James Gunn for several hours and had done "an excellent job." This publicity took effect and Beatrice wrote not long afterwards: "It's fun being spectacular sometimes, but we've all got mountains of crank mail from the exposure"—"What happens when you start blowing up the universe!"—"However this place continues to be delightful, full of peace around and within." In fact she was enjoying being alone, finding herself again after great inner conflict. She didn't know how differently she would feel if she had the children with her, but she was much relieved to hear from a great friend in Dallas that they seemed full of joy and undisturbed.

So started an incredibly productive six months of work at Santa Cruz, which included several trips north to Berkeley near San Francisco and south to Caltech in Pasadena.

I must have questioned a quotation from a talk of hers in one of the reports she had sent us, for she replied: "it may be, as you say, 'bad science' to like the universe being open because it *feels* better, but there is in me a strong delight in that possibility. I think I am tied to the idea of expanding for ever—like life in a sense—more than spatial infinity. In fact more complicated theories are possible, in which the universe is closed spatially, so finite in extent, but will expand for ever. Eddington was wedded philosophically to that model. Currently James Gunn and I are working on the possibility that a model like this really fits the observations best. I'm afraid it's so complicated to get good enough data and bright enough ideas, that we may never feel sure. It amuses me the way scientists' philosophical prejudices colour their arguments. Our friend Jerry Ostriker and I continually accuse each other of making biased scientific arguments because he says I really *want* the universe to be open, and I say he really *wants* it to be closed. Gets us nowhere but makes good parties!"

Reverting to this subject in a later letter she wrote: "You refer, D, to my descriptions of 'human foibles' of my cosmological friends, but in fact I don't think it *is* weakness to be motivated by emotions. What else is the driving force, or the inspiration to think of useful theories? Only if emotional attachment to one's own theory makes one blind to alternatives is it bad. But on the whole I find controversies that I get involved in are stimulating to think the next way to return to the ball, and we all learn what are useful ideas or otherwise as we go."

Friendly discussions also helped develop ideas, as was shown by her description of a visit to Pasadena. "Last weekend, i.e. Thursday until the end of Monday, fitted in between teaching hours here, I was down at Cal Tech. Got a lot of useful work done and went to a large and happy party at the Gunns.

"In fact half of Saturday was taken with helping them cook and half of Sunday (the awake half) was taken up helping them wash bottles, but somehow plenty of science got wedged in as it always does in a place like that.—It's awfully nice having friends among the astronomers all over the country. There are some great people among the best scientists."

Early in March the award of a Sloan fellowship for two years meant "a lot of money (total $19,000 to be managed by Yale) to spend any way I like on research—e.g. financing trips to England in the summer etc." "The Sloan foundation," she explained, "gives out about a dozen a year to young scientists in all fields, generally a few astronomers, so I feel very lucky. It will make a lot of things easier—no haggling with government grants and university administrations for funds for a while."

Her permanent job at Yale, which was definite for five years at least, looked "extremely good from every point of view. So is here and I love California in general and this place in particular, but probably Yale is better academically"—"I wouldn't be happy in every other sort of Paradise if the work environment was poor. It was certainly good at Santa Cruz and, from a researcher's viewpoint even improved before the end of March."

"Teaching is over for the quarter," she wrote, "in fact since I have the next quarter here free of teaching and Yale is giving me the first term (they have long terms) off there, I have no more classes till January. So now research goes on apace and I seem to be writing up months (years on one paper) of work for publication."

Jean Audouze was coming over from France and they had a big review article to put together. Then Jim Gunn was arriving at the end of the week to collaborate on two and two-thirds of large papers (the other third being a student in Austin), as well as on a popular article. At the same time she and Jim were hoping to continue research on the next stage of their big project. "I'm finding the scientific and physical environment here very conducive to thinking original thoughts," she wrote, "really a lovely place. Also the fresh air and exercise (biking and walking) are very good for body and brain."

She had recently bought a bicycle "a toy—which I haven't owned since the old crate I sold for ten shillings on leaving

Christchurch in 1963." It took her 40 minutes to get to the office "up an idyllic little bike track that meanders rather too steeply up through the old farm on the campus with cows getting in the way." She felt humiliated when "younger and fitter characters" passed her on the way up still riding where she had been forced to walk, but "coming home down a similar track takes only about ten minutes, which is a great fun ride. Whiz down hoping there aren't any cows round the corner!"

During April, however, she was in great demand all over the States, speaking at Boulder (Colorado), Sonoma (California), Harvard and Princeton, as well as at an American Physical Society meeting in Washington, D.C.

I was fortunate to catch her in Sant Cruz for a few days on my way to Brazil for a congress of the World Anti-Communist League. It was a thoroughly enjoyable visit among the beautiful surroundings of the campus among the redwoods and the attractive town. A party of Beatrice's friends was a stimulating occasion and most of all I recall with gratitude the final morning. Beatrice was taking me to San Francisco airport and an early start was involved. But when I got up I found her at the dining table with sheets of paper in front of her covered in obscure mathematical calculations. She had been sent an article to review for a scientific journal and had spent over an hour proving that the mathematics on which the author had based his conclusions were inaccurate. It was an astounding display of mental energy, especially as we had been up late the night before.

Some of the places at which she had spoken during April had not greatly impressed her, but she had enjoyed Princeton "scientifically and socially."

"I was invited," she wrote, "to give a seminar at the Institute, which is formal and rather formidable even for an 'informal seminar' in view of a few dominant personalities. I decided to jump right in and talk about the cosmology on my mind, which is evidence that Einstein was wrong—right there in his own place. The result as I hoped was a lot of very interesting suggestions and discussions. It's nice to be beyond being treated as a crank or an upstart!"

"The Washington meeting was an enormous affair, as I thought and my talk generated a lot of interest and a press conference, though the most valuable thing to me, was a chance to talk to some physicists afterwards."

More visits followed to Caltech, San Diego ("smelly smog all

82

the way from Pasadena"), and two trips to Berkeley. Jean Audouze came on a visit and when she took him back to San Francisco airport ("along the coast road with the sea looking gorgeous and white to the horizon; not very pacific") she picked up Dick Larson, "a future colleague at Yale, and brought him back here for the next few days. He's a person who makes me very happy to be going to Yale—extremely nice guy (very shy) and an excellent scientist. He and Sandy (Sandra Faber) and I spent most of three days cooking up new ideas which we hope to get on with in the summer (nearly all best friends will be at Cambridge!)."

This was written at the end of May when her time at Santa Cruz was nearly over. The letter ended: "Now I'm trying to tidy up the loose ends of no fewer than nine papers, which are mostly with various co-authors scattered about in Germany, Texas, Princeton, Pasadena, and even Lick; all suddenly getting finished and out at once before I leave. I don't want to be too tied up when the children are here. Really must censor any new ideas for a few weeks."

The children came and they had a great time together especially on the beaches. When Jim Gunn came up from Caltech, he stayed on specially to join a picnic with the Tinsley and Faber families. But he and Beatrice also worked.

"Jim and I," she wrote, "have about five different papers and projects going, but at last seem to have one both complete and accepted to publication (long and very serious) and another ready to send off (short and rather riskily unorthodox—what I got the last press release for), and two more ready to finish at Cambridge if either of us has time amid the many other projects with people who gather there. I'm partly packed and expecting the furniture movers on Friday. Sad!" The furniture included a beautiful coffee table made from a solid piece of redwood at a small factory which she and I had visited in an inland valley among the trees. "Santa Cruz seems nicer the longer I stay here," she continued. She was writing on June 15th and concluded: "I'll be gone in a week and will try to send you something before I leave for England on the third, if I get across the U.S. as planned."

CHAPTER TEN

Associate Professor at Yale

1975–1978

Beatrice drove the three thousand two hundred miles from Santa Cruz to New Haven by herself. At the end she wrote: "I am rather stiff, sunburnt, and my eyes are tired—otherwise O.K." She had travelled across the Sierras "near Tahoe (snow at road level and gorgeous forest)," down through the deserts of Nevada (with casinos every hundred miles), Salt Flats of Utah, lots of green grass in Wyoming, Nebraska, Iowa and Illinois to Chicago, where she gave herself two nights' rest, staying with her Hungarian friends, the Barnothys. As she reached the city centre "a most torrential thunderstorm with blinding rain" caused her to take a whole hour to reach her host's suburban home, where it had been fine! Pressing on through Indiana, Ohio and a small corner of New York State, she reached New Haven across Connecticut at one o'clock on the day she wrote, six days after she left Santa Cruz. She had never been bored, she stated. It had been "fascinating country all the way" and "shortly after I left California the feeling came over me that I was *going* somewhere rather than leaving somewhere, much to my relief."

Six days later she left for Cambridge after exploring the Yale campus and some of the surrounding country with Richard Larson and feeling "very happy to belong there." She had also found an apartment on tree-lined Whitney Avenue only ten minutes' walk from the Astronomy Department.

In Cambridge a Scottish friend had lent her a flat where there were plenty of astronomy books and gramophone records to interest her. He told her to use his food supplies, which consisted "mostly of Scottish whisky, Scotch shortbread, and Scotch marmalade, Honestly!!" He also told her to use his bicycle which was of a "funny miniature design." It took her into the city in five minutes in one direction and the Institute in five minutes in the other. So she was well set up for the next two months.

These included a visit to Venice, where she was "very moved to be giving a review of cosmology at Hoyle's sixtieth birthday, since it was his books that I read at high school that introduced me to the subject."

On the way back to Cambridge she went to Herstmonceaux Castle in Sussex, where the Royal Greenwich Observatory had been relocated. "It was a dull and pedantic meeting, unfortunately, but I made the most of people there to spend lots of time talking to them, which is generally the best part of a conference anyway. People are so much more approachable at the breakfast table or over a drink after dinner than in their offices."

After that she was "supposed to be planning" another conference in Cambridge "but," she wrote, "we're leaving it as informal as possible to promote new ideas." It turned out "a very productive little 'workshop' conference. About fifty people all very much in the same kind of work." There was also "a lot of socialising, going out to dinner, sitting around at pubs by the Campus all the evening. (It has been incredibly hot and 101% humid).—I seemed to have all my favourite people (astronomers at least) in one place, and was very happy. My great friend Sandy Faber from Lick came for the week and we had a very good time together. She is a friend I will miss going away."

She was trying to finish papers she had started at Santa Cruz, including a review article with Jean Audouze, who came over from France. "Several 'pundits' from around the Institute were reading the first draft and providing useful criticism.—I wish it wasn't so hot."

It cooled off at the end of August, when James Gunn had come over from California with his wife. The review with Jean Audouze was finished, so the four of them went out to "a rather elegant pub for dinner," and then to a fair on Midsummer Common where they chased each other round in Dodgem Cars. Jean did not enjoy it; he said it reminded him too much of Paris traffic!

Beatrice herself celebrated the cooler weather by taking a long bike ride into the country to watch the start of harvesting. She had been working on more cosmology with Jim, but they "kept having new ideas and not finishing." Then, just before returning to New Haven, she was invited by Richard Gott, a young American who was a visiting Fellow at Trinity College, to go to dinner in the hall there. "Richard gave me an historical tour," she wrote, "including echoes in the cloister where Newton first measured the speed of sound."

Back in New Haven she soon settled into her new job. "Yale," she wrote, "is proving a very pleasant place to work. There are really nice people in the astronomy department here, and an extraordinary absence of bad feelings amongst them. This year there are two new young people (junior lecturer level), both of whom I met in California in 1972—one was an extremely good student of Jim Gunn's—and they and my old colleague Dick Larson from here are forming a gang that I think will do much useful astronomy.—Another fun thing is that this year (i.e., till June) I'm responsible for getting visiting speakers each week, which means I can organise visits from people I want to see."

What added to her enjoyment of Yale was the amount of music. Richard Larson was a cellist and took her to a recital of Brahms' cello sonatas. Then, after taking tickets for a series of concerts by visiting artists, she wrote "I must get playing again. The longer I don't practice, the more I dread starting up again."

A furniture salesman amused her by saying "They've found the universe is even bigger than they can ever measure or something." His remark, she was sure, arose from publicity given to one of her lectures, though she did not tell him who she was. The same publicity had also resulted in an invitation to talk to a conference of science reporters. "Sounds fun," she commented.

The autumn came and "living with red oak leaves and chestnuts and poplar smells in the air" was "very nostalgic of Christchurch. It's strangely like a full circle of life—starting a new long term of life here, whereas in Christchurch every autumn felt like a new start. I have a sense of hope and power over the future that has escaped me for years."

As it turned out the future at Yale was to be only five and a half years, no longer than Beatrice's time in Christchurch.

But the sense of hope and power, with which they started, found fulfillment in considerable achievement.

On the last day of September the little gang of like-minded astronomers drove up into Vermont. It was a glorious day and they picnicked by a flooded stream looking across the forest "stretching for a hundred miles across the mountains in every imaginable shade of red, purple, orange and yellow with dark patches of pine and fir for contrast." They dined at a little restaurant in Massachusetts, getting home well after dark, when she sat down to write to us. Next morning early she was off to Philadelphia to lecture to a group of physicists and astronomers. "Life," she wrote, "is very good," and what made it even better was that she was starting playing chamber music again, and her mind was "very absorbed in new astronomical ideas, which are likely to turn into lengthy projects."

A committee was formed at Yale to improve the status of women in the University and Beatrice joined it. So she "felt obliged to go to hear the University President speaking on the subject. He said all the right things in a little too polished a way, so it all seemed rather condescending. It's going to be hard to think of good solutions to the problems, and it isn't made any easier by the militant feminists or by suave conservatives." However she was sure she wouldn't meet the hostility she encountered in Dallas to women with "genuine grievances," and I think she must have lost interest in the whole subject, as it is not mentioned again in her letters, and there was never a sign at Yale of discrimination against her personally.

When November came she went to Harvard to a meeting where James Gunn was a special guest. As usual they were at work on a joint paper, and one of their recent efforts had made "a spate of notoriety to which Sullivan" (the science writer for the *New York Times*) "added, including quoting some Plato that we used in our preface to the paper. Jim escaped from the meeting straight up Mt. Palomar observing, but I've been besieged by phone calls etc. etc. including yesterday a telephone interview with the Canadian Broadcasting Company. Funnily it's by no means the most significant piece of work I've done, but it captures the public imagination more than most things. Fun being famous for a little while! Sometimes I remember in a rather startled way how I used to read the encyclopedia as a kid and wish I could understand and contribute to cosmology."

Alan and Terry came for the Thanksgiving holiday which

meant a week virtually off work, but immediately afterwards there were two official visitors to cope with and a couple of T.V. programmes to record with Bill van Altena, the chairman of the Astronomy Department. "It was rather fun," Beatrice wrote, "although the interviewer knew pathetically little about science and asked lots of inappropriate questions. It was often hard not to laugh at their irrelevance."

The publicity following the Harvard meeting, which reached not only the *New York Times* but even *Der Spiegel*, finally resulted in the *Scientific American* asking for an article. Beatrice considered that "by far the best generalists' science publication there is," so she and James Gunn collaborated with two other astronomers to produce an article "with literary help from Rosemary Gunn," thinking it was a chance "to teach our stuff to the general public." Beatrice undertook to edit the final version and as late as the following January was spending many hours on the phone with co-authors in Chicago, Kentucky and California. In the end she achieved an agreed result, she stated!

The first term of 1976 saw her undertaking a course for undergraduates. "What a pleasure," she wrote, "after the University of Texas undergrads. There, they include almost anyone who can get through high school, and many take astronomy as a supposedly easy way of fulfilling science requirements. But at Yale the undergrads are a highly selected bunch, and I'm teaching the most stringent of three introductory astronomy courses, so they're really interested in science and enjoy mathematics."

But the course had not been going for long, when Alan was rushed to hospital in Dallas with a huge growth in his chest. It was not malignant as it turned out, but a very big operation was involved to remove a teratoma, a rare form of growth which can be fatal unless taken away. Beatrice waited in anxiety, first to hear whether cancer was involved and then, when the operation was over, till it would not cause alarm to Terry or Alan himself for an absent mother to arrive at his hospital bed. Finally, she flew to Dallas, and found Alan still in intensive care "with countless tubes and monitors on him, but being marvellously philosophical." His attitude no doubt contributed to an amazingly fast recovery and it was not long before he had even returned to playing soccer. But at this time Beatrice told her sister Theodora she was "quite exhausted emotionally and physically."

After some unseasonable warmth it began to snow again in

New Haven in early March and Beatrice wrote that it would be a preparation for the Swiss Alps. She was going as a teacher to an astronomy school at a place called Saas-Fee, eighteen hundred metres up in the mountains of the Canton of Valais. It turned out to be "the loveliest place I can imagine coming to teach astronomy, not to mention astronomy is the nicest thing I can think of doing while not walking in the Alps." There were some sixty students, some of them rather senior astronomers. The two other teachers were Richard Larson, a Canadian, and an Australian, an old friend of Beatrice's. All the lectures were in English, but the students had to contend with a variety of accents, including Beatrice's Kiwi—spoken at a speed which, she said, she could not control! Outside the lectures however a multitude of tongues was to be heard, and she wrote of spending "hours talking with the participants in mixtures of English, French and Italian (I give up on German)." Evidently the Science German course, which she had taken at Canterbury University at the insistence of Dr. Metcalf, had not resulted in conversational fluency.

The whole week was idyllic. "Never did I dream," she wrote, "that I'd be invited to teach a course like this in a place like this. It's funny to find myself an authority in the field, but very rewarding."

There was one slight contretemps. She and Richard had driven up from Geneva in a hired car, which had to be left in a car park on the edge of the village, as no cars were allowed in the streets. A day or two later some German tourists alleged, quite untruly, that they had damaged their Volkswagen. The two-man police force carried out an examination for scraped paint etc., but seemed to be more impressed by being told by the conference organiser that she and Richard were distinguished foreign astronomers! Anyhow the Germans were dismissed and left the village unplacated. Richard thought the whole incident a huge joke, but Beatrice stated that they were relieved at the end of the school to get out of the village without one of the two police stopping them!

On returning to Yale Beatrice found life too full for writing up results of research or playing the violin for some while. Rowena came from Venezuela to stay with her and James Gunn arrived as a special lecturer, invited by the students, who were allowed to ask one visitor a year. Beatrice gave a party for staff and students whom he knew, some two dozen people in all. But she said it was "not too much effort, since my style of party is to get wine, beer, nuts and cheese and let people swallow them while talking."

A return to research became possible at the end of May, when classes ceased. Jean Audouze came over once more and they corrected proofs of a long joint paper. But her own work was often interrupted by going to talk in other places. Even Beatrice complained of too much traveling, when she had been to Washington and back in one day, and on the next afternoon, set off for Austin. However "visiting the old haunts at Austin stirred up no nostalgia at all. I had a pleasant talk with Harlan Smith, a set of disagreements with the old French astronomer, fun giving a lecture in the afternoon and a friendly dinner with some old buddies."

Spring brought "fabulous weather and flowers and trees" to Connecticut. Beatrice spent one whole afternoon alone "walking in a nearby wild park admiring dogwoods and new maple leaves, then in a damp forest a few miles with a little brook in rushing torrents." After that a day in the big city to the south, with its smog and grime, made her exclaim "I hate New York." At the start of June she was up at Aspen in the Colorado mountains with the children, taking part in astronomical discussions, while they climbed around the rocks. When she returned to Yale the department had moved into new premises and she found to her delight that from her new and larger office she looked out into the tops of old oak trees. Natural surroundings were always of great importance to her.

At the end of the month she gave a talk to a big Astronomical Society meeting at "an idyllic small college in Haverford, Pennsylvania. It was quite an effort," she commented, but seemed to be greeted well—"Now it will be peace and quiet and preparing for the I.A.U. in France."

But the peace and quiet was relative, because of the American Bicentennial ("buycentennial," Beatrice called it in a bracket). The preparations she had found tiresome, but when the time came she enjoyed some varied concerts and the "spectacular fireworks" over the harbour. There she and a friend were so completely parked in that they had to walk home, fetching the car later! At the same time "the whole countryside" was "full of chamber music," for which she went to Marlboro in Vermont and a country estate in northern Connecticut.

On August the first she left for a month in Britain where

she gave an invited lecture at Cambridge and managed to fit in a visit to friends in Edinburgh before going to France for a meeting of two thousand astronomers at Grenoble where she again spoke. She also caught her first cold for three years on a beautiful but wet expedition which included a damp picnic under some trees by a river! It was a cold that every astronomer seemed to develop due to "wet and stuffy rooms together" she commented!

A four-day gap before another meeting in Paris allowed a motor drive with friends down to the Italian lakes over the Col de Cenis, then up through Switzerland, "looking most gorgeous, mile after mile of green valleys and blue lakes, houses covered with geraniums, orchards and mountains sometimes emerging," then into Liechtenstein, where they spent a night, followed by another in Morat. Both places came out of "story books." It was a wonderful time of refreshment before going on to Paris, where she enjoyed staying with the Audouze family, but found it "a bit of a hassle fighting train crowds for nearly an hour twice each day to get to the meetings." These, as often, were less rewarding than the conversations; but she loved seeing Paris again and spent a whole day sightseeing with James Gunn. Then on her way home to America, she stopped in London to see Nannie Gullidge, and was relieved to find her looking better than on previous visits, though sadly lonely in her retirement. She urged me to write more often to the old lady.

Back at Yale there were fresh research projects, a fresh bunch of students and more speaking engagements to fulfill. An added responsibility was organising an international conference of astronomers in her field of work to be held in the following May.

Mattie and I were planning a further trip to the U.S. and Britain in 1977, but in November 1976 we found that Beatrice was already so booked up that it would be useless to try to visit her on our way to Britain and the days would have to be carefully chosen if we meant to see her on our way back!

In December "life had been awfully busy, though mostly with pleasant things." One of them was a "monstrous meeting in Boston, 600 people, successor to the gathering in Dallas just before I left at the end of 1974. I had to give a talk—a very popular and inevitably gee-whizzy review on cosmology (the State of the Universe address as it was dubbed by a reviewer last time, when someone else did it). I still felt as though I just spent the whole summer at conferences, so I drove up and back (3 hours each way) in one long day, with a student to keep me company and awake!!"

After that the Astronomy Department Christmas party put on by students was light relief. "As always they entertained the faculty, this time with a play called 'Gone with the stellar wind.' I was Scarlet O'Tinsley, who had to preserve her plantation in order to find out whether the universe would expand for ever. Quite a role to live down! The rest of my colleagues were cast as combinations of themselves and characters in the book, played by various students. At the end I won a lot of money and announced I would now get famous by solving the problems of cosmology, but the rest of the cast shouted back in chorus, 'Frankly, my dear, we don't give a damn!' Much fun!"

The new year started bitterly cold, and with snowdrifts blocking the drains, the avenue became up to six inches deep in water when they melted. Beatrice felt lucky not having to take the car out to go to work. She was as busy as ever, but happy that another violinist had joined their small chamber music group. "At last I'm playing string quartets again, which include most of my favourite chamber music."

Lectures away from Yale before term started including two at the Goddard Space Flight Center and one each at Johns Hopkins University in Baltimore and at a local astronomers' meeting. In addition she was supplying ideas to a small team working on a camera project for a large telescope to be flown on a satellite "some time in the political never, never."

Preparations for the May conference elicited the comment: "The great and famous speakers are largely temperamental prima donnas. I hope I never become one!—More grey hairs every day." Mattie and I were on the move during the next months and I have no record of the conference itself, only a comment at the start of July that it had left her "collapsed." By then, however, she had almost finished putting "the proceedings, including twenty hours of discussions into a book" and was "looking forward to getting back to hours of original science." The book was printed speedily, and by August the 5th she could report that it was "now out, and with most of the mailing and advertising handled the burden of all that seems to be over."

Alan and Terry came to stay and then went to a nearby summer camp where she went to see them and finally fetched them away, just before she left on the last day of August for

93

meetings at Bonn in West Germany, Torun and Poland and Tallin in Estonia. "The Bonn one," she wrote, "is actually being held at Bad Munstereifel, which looks like a most delightful spot. The costs are using up my Sloan grant of two years ago fast, which is what it was intended for. Most international meetings can't pay travel expenses, although some cover living costs, and I'm glad to say that the Estonian Academy of Sciences is doing so, since the Intourist Hotel is astronomical in cost."

She returned to New Haven on September 19th, just in time to welcome us on the 22nd. I shall not forget our rendezvous at Kennedy Airport. Beatrice drove down from Connecticut, I flew from Venezuela, where I had been visiting Rowena, and Mattie arrived from London, all within half an hour of each other. It seems miraculous that nothing went wrong with the arrangements, as hour long delays over Kennedy were all too common at the time! We drove to New Haven up a freeway lined with trees for most of the way.

It was a happy visit, shortened to six days by Beatrice having an engagement in Toronto. Besides having a good time in Yale, we drove up to Vermont for a night to see the fall colours and a play by Eugene O'Neill in a delightful small theatre at Marlboro. There was as yet no cloud on Beatrice's horizon, and we were all happy when we also flew to Toronto and on to visit friends near Stratford, Ontario.

Beatrice followed up the Toronto meeting by driving herself to Washington in her new car, and, after a quiet Christmastide, filled with research and music, she paid a friendly visit to the Barnothys in Chicago before going on to a three-day meeting in Austin.

February was ushered in with New Haven's worst blizzard in ninety years, and the army being sent in to "dig out" the town. "There's a great pile of snow being built outside my place," wrote Beatrice, "and a terrible noise of heavy earth moving equipment." Then, before the end of the month came a letter with very disquieting news. "I'm in for a rather unpleasant week, sorry to say. A lump on my leg had turned out to be skin cancer, and they want to excise a rather larger piece than can be done under local anaesthetic. So I'm going into hospital on Tuesday. It's going to involve a skin graft, so I expect to be limping for a while." However, she expected to be out of the actual hospital within a week and into the Yale Health Center, "a nice place on the campus where my friends can visit me."

Her "marvellous friends" had taken over her various duties, as well as collecting her mail and giving her human support. She hadn't phoned us, she stated, to save us worry, but gave us a number in the astronomy department to ring for information about her progress. "I expect to be back at work by April 1st at *latest*. Meanwhile we played lovely trios last night."

She was able to climb the stairs to her apartment by March 29th, and the doctor was pleased with her graft, though she thought it looked atrocious, and she had some nagging sores in the donor area. There was also a large incision at the top of her leg where they had taken away the lymph nodes. But she was planning to go to California early in May, and the first week of April she started "taking classes sitting in front of an overhead projector." "Every day I manage a little more before the system says "rest." Total inactivity for eleven days is a large part of the problem ... muscular weakness."

With stern realism she gave away all her skirts and dresses that did not cover the knees, and was compelled to limit her driving to short distances around the town. But she had more offers of lifts than she could accept, and all sorts of other offers of help.

I planned to visit her as soon as possible, and she warned me to be sure I had adequate medical insurance. The three days she had been in hospital just for tests had run up a bill for $1,000. "Luckily," she wrote, "Yale employees have comprehensive insurance and I won't pay a penny as far as I know." As it turned out the bill for the actual operation arrived when I was there. It was over $8,000! Almost all of it was cancelled out by the insurance, but for some reason neither of us understood, Beatrice was called upon to pay somewhere about $8.00.

My visit took place in early May. Beatrice had not fully recovered from the operation but was not noticeably handicapped. As we had arranged she did not meet me at La Guardia airport, but she was able to drive her car out of town to a small park for her voice to be recorded for a T.V. script in a place hopefully free of town noises. She also drove me up a hill outside the town, where there was real quiet and a wonderful view and the summit was covered with kalmia bushes. We talked at length and Beatrice seemed not so concerned for herself as for her students, specially those not doing so well. In particular there was a girl, who had given a lame excuse for not sitting an exam and was threatening to sue the department for not passing her! After I left she wrote telling more about the students. In particular "the girl, who caused the trouble by not coming, has sobered up and is trying to be nice to us all and will try again in September. Things have all calmed down."

In June Richard Larson drove her down to the University of Maryland, where a meeting of some two hundred astronomers included Australians and two Estonians she had met in Tallin, who brought her as a present a record of early music she had heard at a concert there. Altogether she thought she knew about a quarter of the astronomers present.

On their return to Yale Beatrice found that her promotion to a full professorship with tenure had become official. "Everyone (specially me) is very pleased," she wrote.

CHAPTER ELEVEN

Yale Professor with Tenure

1978–1981

It was mid-August before Beatrice received official notice of her promotion, but, as she wrote, "more tangible evidence was last month's pay cheque!" Neither the promotion nor the operation seemed to make any difference to her activities.

In early July Alan and Terry came to stay for a fortnight, then she went back to research and visited Santa Cruz for an astronomers' meeting. She stayed with the Fabers and their two daughters in their large house, and it was "beautiful once the fog lifted." Back at Yale at the end of August she was trying to finish a paper, but "business" was starting up again with a new term. "I hope the new students don't have any problem personalities!" she wrote. "We're about to hold the oral exam for the woman Daddy may remember, who didn't turn up for very petty reasons. The problem man is back too, noisy as ever, and trying everyones patience. At least my colleagues agree with me that they are hard to get on with!" A new faculty member had been a student at Santa Cruz when she was there, and she was hoping that his pianist wife would fit in with the astronomers' music group.

After the term started she wrote: "Even though I'm not teaching a course this term I will be very busy with students and other duties—i.e., occupations other than research, which is what I want to spend most of my time on! I now have three PhD theses to supervise, and two term projects, as well as the non-scientific business of all graduate students. Hopefully I've had the last of set backs medically for a *while*. Today was the last in the series of vaccinations, so when I've recovered from feeling wuzzy (in a few days) that should be the end of it; except for various x-rays for a year or more."

In spite of not having a course to take she found herself "running round in circles with odd jobs," and having to give evenings to research, though a certain amount of music was fitted in.

Restrictions on the distance she could drive had been cancelled. One Saturday she drove herself even farther north in Vermont than she had taken us in the previous fall. "I took along my new pocket camera," she wrote, and "if the first film is bad it won't be for want of a suitable subject for coloured pictures."

She had bought the camera for use in Australia and New Zealand at the end of the year, but before going away, she made quick trips to Princeton and New York in her own car to speak at the University and a research center. She also "had a quick trip across the sound to Stony Brook on Long Island—via a great company called New Haven Airways. It was a tiny plane going over—four small passenger seats and two pilots seats with no partition—and there was only me and the pilot in it. Coming back it was an eight seater with three passengers. The weather was rather hazy, but still it was a lot of fun, (purpose being to talk to some astronomers there)."

Ten days later she flew to Sydney and Canberra for astronomical work, and on December 1st reached Invercargill for a three-day visit to her sister Theodora and family. Then she came on to Wellington to attend an astronomers' meeting. She stayed with us for four days and her programme allowed for some leisure. I have a snapshot of her taken down by the Cook Straits against a background of rocks and sea. Her hair is blown about by the wind and only her glasses could suggest she was a distinguished professor!

Writing from Yale again just after Christmas, she asked for photographs of herself as a child which might show the place where the cancer had developed. Some doctors in New Haven were making a special study of melanoma, trying to find out if it could be detected early. As it turned out the photographs showed nothing at all, but Beatrice remarked that, if she had to develop melanoma, she could not have done so in a better place

98

than Yale, though that was hardly a good reason for becoming a professor there!

The girl who had been given a second chance to take the course was soon causing trouble again, appealing against the decision to fail her, and making incredible accusations which Beatrice had to spend a whole afternoon refuting. Beatrice was afraid that if the Dean denied her appeal she would take Yale to court!

In the New Year Beatrice spent a day in Houston and returned to Yale to start teaching a course for graduates. She had had a series of X-rays and "come through clear—so I can go on assuming the cancer was completely cured. There's no point in living as though it wasn't anyway." A busy time followed with teaching and administrative duties connected with finding money for new students, not to mention a visit from James Gunn for work on a project. But she fitted in a flying visit to Britain, whence a postcard simply described the meeting she attended as interesting. London was under snow.

She was deeply concerned about the plight of the former caretaker of the apartment building on Whitney Avenue, whose children had become great friends with Alan and Terry. One of them had suffered an eye injury in an attack by a fellow pupil and the headmaster, whom Beatrice stigmatised as one of the local mafia, refused to investigate the matter properly. The other children were also being victimised at school, apparently for being Italians—so the family went to New York and fell into the clutches of a criminal employer there. They had then returned to New Haven penniless and unable to get employment benefit, because the New York employer, who had actually been put on some criminal charge, refused to give the father a character. Beatrice was sure the matter would right itself eventually when the law took its course, and she proved right in the end. But meanwhile mother, father and six children were virtually starving. So she lent them money and did what she could to help. "What a wicked world," she wrote, "and social system!"

Then in April she told us "the doctors are becoming rather more suspicious about the state of my cancer. I'm having a lot of X-rays and similar tests, but nothing has been decided about treatment yet and there isn't likely to be any sudden change in my life. Ever since the operation I've known there was a fifty-fifty chance of recurrence, so, if it happens, I feel much better prepared emotionally than I was for the original news."

A week later she had minor surgery to remove a suspicious lump from under the skin on "the same old leg." It was almost certainly recurrence of the same cancer "but so localised it is by no means certain that the disease is systemic." "Between trips to the hospital where I get a lot of useful reading done in waiting rooms," she added, "it's been a nice busy week.—I've been writing astronomy all day. Spring is really here, with flowers and greenery sprouting everywhere."

A fortnight later, when she had been very busy with visitors, she was told by the doctors that the lump had been a recurrence of melanoma, "which means that last year's operation didn't cure it. (It was only a bare fifty percent chance anyway). There is now quite a strong chance of further recurrences, so I'm starting on drug treatments, which mean several visits to the hospital's cancer clinic every month. I expect to feel unwell for a few days, but all their two dozen patients on this regimen are working normally."

So she continued her busy schedule "doing what I like best, working out new things and writing papers. Six of the students are about to finish their theses, and three have very good jobs indeed, others O.K." "The spring is gorgeous, all dogwoods and lilacs by now. I've been enjoying everything and the drug treatments are pretty tolerable."

She had sent us an article with an accompanying photo, for which she apologised as no longer like her. "The article isn't a bad description of the line of research I enjoy most. It's funny to realize that my thesis work, which is now regarded as a useful step forward in astronomy, was generally regarded as impossible speculation at the time!"

June was occupied by students from as far away as California and Texas consulting her about their theses, and by a visit from Alan and Terry, during which she went to Wellesley outside Boston to give a talk, taking Terry with her for company on the drive. Friends took care of the children when she went to hospital for drug treatments, and Richard took them to a restaurant on the day when one of them always made her sick. During a week free of drugs she took the children to Cape Cod and the Acadia National Park in Maine. "I thought I would never see so much beautiful country outside New Zealand" she commented.

When the children had left, she set off for three days in the French Alps, lecturing at a summer school at Les Houches, followed by a day in Amsterdam, and two at the observatory at Groningen. "It's easy enough for me to escape from the doctor and nurses for a week," she wrote, "because I go in normally once a week, three successive days the next, once the next week, and not at all the fourth. They've been able to schedule everything so as not to spoil my summer plans hardly at all. This goes on until another recurrence (or unless), which would be much more serious."

The trip to Europe was brief but enjoyable. The little town of Les Houches near Chamonix had a spectacular view and she had time in Amsterdam to visit the "marvellous" Van Gogh museum. Then she was given a "lively time" by the astronomers at Groningen.

Back at Yale, however, treatments did interfere with work, when James Gunn could only come to collaborate on their large project during her worst week. But she did manage a visit to Princeton and the greater part of an International Astronomical Union meeting in Montreal, which Beatrice considered too long and too big, with two thousand attending. Even after a week she kept running across people she did not know were there.

Her routine visits to hospital for treatments she called "quite efficient, because the nurses handle everything, but when I have to see a doctor I can wait for hours (as yesterday: two hours of useful reading)." The treatments were planned to last two years unless there was another tumour. "Meanwhile, anyway, I concentrate on everything else possible, and there is plenty to enjoy."

September saw the arrival of new students, all of whom seemed "to be nice people; at least no sign of disastrous personalities!" Beatrice was preparing a new graduate course. To her delight an excellent pianist had joined the chamber music group, so good that she feared the lady might find their standard too amateur. However she herself felt encouraged to do more practising and was finding the improvement in technique "very rewarding." The group had enjoyed a lively evening playing piano quintets.

By the middle of the month it was decided to reduce her drug treatments, "a welcome let up." The doctor also told her, "after a long talk about the worst and best course of the disease," that it was most unlikely that she "would not be able to be responsible for an 11-year-old until June." So she agreed enthusiastically to take Terry to live with her for the rest of her school year. Brian and Yvon had had a son, and with Alan and her own daughter, Courtenay, to care for, Yvon was finding the exceedingly active Terry too much of a handful. Beatrice sent her to a private school with small classes, and wrote that she had guarantees of help with Terry when she herself was sick from medicines. Terry's only condition for coming to New Haven was that she should be allowed to bring her hamster!

The new regime started happily, but at the beginning of December Beatrice had to return to hospital for the removal of "cancerous lymph nodes, still very localised, which is encouraging." Seven of her students came to visit her, which she found cheering, and she was soon released and put on a slightly different treatment, "luckily with a drug that is less nauseating than the last one."

The student's party that year was "a take off of Star Trek, with all the faculty somehow involved and some tremendously good impersonations; I still giggle at the thought of it," she wrote.

As Christmas approached she felt normal enough to walk around doing Christmas shopping. The new chemotherapy was relatively painless, the stitches were out and the scar healing well. In fact she was assuming that the new treatment would be totally successful, because "there isn't much point in doing otherwise."

So the year ended happily, especially as the Metcalfs came to stay for a few days. "We played piano quartets together, very reminiscent of old times. They are such lovely people."

The first letter in the new year was written "early in the morning" before "taking Terry to the bus to start the new term and back to being in the office by 7:30 for me!" When the Yale term began she started going to town three mornings a week to teach a class of undergraduates. The surgeon had told her she was very well after the last operation and that she needn't see him for six months "unless something else crops up." But she was still taking drugs and there was talk of her having radiation treatment, which would involve daily visits to the hospital. "Thank goodness," she wrote, "the insurance, through Yale, pays for all this!"

By the end of the month she had decided herself to take the radiation course "after extensive consultation, reading the research etc," although she "got the jitters at the thought of lying under a 4 MeV accelerator." "The idea is that if the cancer is confined to that area (by surgical scars), the radiation should finish it off. The problems are that the melanoma cells could have got away, in which case it's locking the stable door after the horse has fled, and that melonoma is very very resistive to radiation." She appreciated getting to know "an admirable and very nice group of doctors (also Yale professors) who have discovered how to use certain high doses to shrink melanoma tumours. I don't have a tumour, so it is sheer conjecture that the same dose could kill off a small number of cancer cells—I think it would be silly not to try." "There was a stunning piano concert on Tuesday night."

Then she and Terry got the 'flu' and the hamster was "sometimes the liveliest creature about the house." But, with other staff ill, and in spite of hospital visits every afternoon, Beatrice kept up on her teaching schedule and the supervision of decisions "on admitting new students for next year."

Every letter was full of Terry's progress at school and with her swimming and roller skating. Her mid-term report was the best she ever had, so they had gone out to dinner with Richard, "a great friend of Terry's and very good for her." She and Terry were getting on really well together, and "very little friction, and for every reason I'm glad that she's here."

At the end of February she went to speak at a public meeting in Massachusetts, and, during March after a visit from James Gunn to discuss their joint research, she flew to Austin for a meeting, leaving Terry at Dallas en route for a visit to the rest of the family.

At the end of April a congress of the Anglican Fellowship of Prayer was held in New Haven, so I combined attending it with seeing Beatrice. With Terry in her apartment, I booked in at the hotel where the congress was being held a few days before it started. Richard Larson drove Beatrice, Terry and myself out into a forest, where there was a small lake and Terry played in the sand beside it while we talked. Another day Beatrice took me once more up the hill with the kalmia bushes, and there we had what turned out to be our last long conversation. She was aware, she said, that ten years were the very most she could hope to live, and she very much wanted to see five of them to make sure that Terry got to university. She was sure the girl had a very good brain, but needed the stimulus to concentrate, which she was the best person to give. This was clearly of more concern to her than her research, or even her own life!

On the day the congress ended she came with Terry to fetch me and we went to see a small street where white cherry trees were in extraordinary bloom, then on to the seaside, where my last photo of her was taken, as before in Wellington, beside rocks and sea. We said goodbye in New Haven's unromantic railway station, whence I took a train to Philadelphia to visit friends. Then I went on to Stevenson outside Baltimore to the country home of my friend of half a century, Helen Shoemaker, one of the founders of the Anglican Fellowship of Prayer. In that setting, in the peaceful old house with the great trees around it and a chance to dig in the soil, I could recover from the unsettling sadness in which my parting with Beatrice had left me.

Beatrice herself was feeling well, and looking for a larger apartment in order to house Terry more spaciously. Alan came to stay and they all went for a bit of a climb after which Beatrice had to admit she had overexerted herself. However, she went to an American Astronomical Society meeting and came home with a sore thigh, which was not improved by rowing the children on the lake. She had to return to the Yale Infirmary, "spending three hours being seen by a total of six doctors," who had varied opinions "though none of them seemed to think there was any recurrence of cancer." The children had to be sent off to Texas, "very unhappy at leaving me." Richard saw them off, before organising a gang of students to complete the move into the new apartment, which was located in the next block.

Beatrice stayed in the infirmary for nine days, occupying a private room till the new apartment could be made habitable. Physical treatment cleared up the inflammation, though it was still undiagnosed. The general belief was that it had been a side effect of the radiation treatment. "So," she wrote, "I needn't worry that it was anything worse."

So, after allowing herself just time to appreciate the extra space in the new apartment, she sent Terry to a summer camp, got a student to care for the hamster and flew off to Cambridge once again. Before leaving she wrote "I'm still trying to cut down on physical exertion. England is not the easiest country to be lazy and comfortable in! At least I expect it to be a lot cooler."

This time she had rooms in the college called Trinity Hall "with a very soggy bed and ill-kept bathroom facilities down the hall; but it felt very much like being at Cambridge, with a rose garden and pigeons outside." "The meeting was a lot of fun, interesting papers, many interesting people and lots of really good friends. There was a spare week-end, but I was pretty tired and spent most of it sitting in the beautiful garden reading." Her sole contact with relatives was a phone call to her godmother, Aunt Patsy, and she was back in New Haven after three weeks.

Then the inflammation returned and she was forced "to be rather lazy," but still found herself quickly tired because of anaemia caused by her medicine, "they may reduce the dose to help out." Mercifully, when the students returned she was given a small workload, and had no course to teach, but soon she had to reduce it further. On September 27th we heard: "I haven't written for a while because of more medical problems namely continued anaemia and time consuming blood transfusions plus a series of tests. The anaemia is levelling off, i.e., I retained the blood count better after a transfusion and I won't be getting any more of the medicine that caused it. (Thank goodness) However, the other tests have brought bad news, I can't think of anything better than to tell it to you all at once. Yesterday I was told that I have tumours in the lungs and liver. The liver disease is the more serious. It's course is quite unpredictable in an individual case, but typically patients succumb in six to twelve months. So far I feel O.K. except for a nagging pain in the side. That isn't really surprising, and in fact it has been the most probable course of events since the original tumour on my right leg two and a half years ago, but still ... it is a shock. My friends can be counted on to do everything possible, especially Richard, who has totally committed himself to caring for me and Terry. She will probably start boarding school when I get disabled, but so far she and I support each other well most of the time. Please, I don't want you to come rushing out to see me. I would *much* rather you remember all the good times we've had together, and not to see me as a terminal cancer patient."

So, after all, she was not going to have her five years to see Terry through to university. A fortnight later she wrote again: "On the whole I'm feeling better because my blood has recovered, and it will probably remain O.K., since I've gone off chemotherapy. We're having some perfectly beautiful autumn weather and the maple trees all round are turning wonderful reds, so its not hard to enjoy life. Richard made a great decision to move in with me and Terry to help us look after ourselves, which he certainly does. What a really marvellous friend he is! Of course I've known that for nearly five years, but not every friendship is put to such a test. It's kind of funny and ironic that we should be living together under these circumstances, after deciding for so long that we preferred to live separately (a simple reason for not getting married in case you wondered), but it will work out very well.—Did I tell you that I am also extremely happy with the doctor who is now in charge of me, my primary doctor from the Yale health services?"

Writing again, only four days later, when we had spoken on the phone, she explained that the doctor was also the medical director of the familiar Yale Infirmary and "says they often have terminal patients there—among the cheerful students with athletic injuries etc! and pride themselves on a 'hospice' atmosphere. It's good to know all that's available if necessary." Meanwhile she was on 24-hour rather strong pain relievers which made her alternatively sleepy and lively. She was spending four to five hours a day at work, "some of that time sleeping at my desk! But the waking hours are reasonably comfortable."

She even managed to go to a concert with Richard, "tiring but worth it! Of course he was the first person to know when I got cancer and we've been through countless emotions over it all together since 1978. I don't know how I would have come through the whole scene without him."

Soon she was back in a private room in the infirmary with friends and students as constant visitors. She even managed to finish a research paper there, the last of nearly a hundred. Perhaps, even in her own opinion, she had finished her contribution to cosmology, for she had told me once that all mathematicians did their best work before they were forty and she became forty in the following January.

I do not have her letters for several months, but I recall that the time came when she wrote that her life would be measured in weeks or even days. Fortunately there was a telephone by her bed and we were able to talk about once a fortnight from then on. She had lost the use of her right hand, but she managed to send a Christmas card written with the left hand, and by February she sent a long letter which began by stating that she had got "pretty fast" at writing that way.

I had telephoned to her after driving up from Invercargill via the Lindis Pass and Lakes Pukaki and Tekapo, and she began her letter by recalling the "unbeatable beauty of New Zea-

106

land." Then she expressed concern about proposed cuts in child nutrition and heating fuel programs in the United States. "There's little enough social justice already in this country" she wrote.

Only then turning to more personal matters she described Terry as "very loving and nice when she visits and we play dominos and scrabble. But she's very nervous about my state. (It's been a long strain on her and others knowing I was expected to die before Christmas, and not having any idea what to expect now.) Richard is a pillar of strength and he's wonderfully understanding of Terry."

"Rowena," she added, "has been calling me every week or two. She found a crazy phone that gives you three minutes of international talk for one coin, then gives back the coin after cutting off! But we can only talk for three minutes because there's always a long impatient queue for the phone."

She asked me to share the letter with Theodora and David. "I don't have enough news to write any more letters." Rowena's crazy Venezuelan telephone was soon mended and she could not afford further calls. So, as was her habit, she expressed her feelings in verse, writing in Spanish, which had evidently become instinctive to her. I quote some of the translation she made herself:

> The solstice has fallen
> behind, and I don't know
> if you've died or are staying
> on time's defile
>
> My hand punishes itself
> with cuts for the paralysis
> of your ending.
>
> It seems our footprints
> diverge since we dug
> in the garden to get to
> Australia or Hell
>
> You followed the precision
> of baroque music to the limit
> of the measurable cosmos
> and spoke of the beginning

and of the end—I drill
through the floors of memory
groping after origins
and laws of growth.

The betrayal of blackened
cells is taking you—
Sometimes I stand at the door
of the reflecting chamber

The light dilates.
Is it you seeing
through my eyes in passing
out of time?

Where there are no longer
eyes or memory
our forces will flow in the same universe.

Beatrice wrote once more and I treasure the note, written on a card showing all the signs of the zodiac, again, of course, with her left hand. "Dear Daddy and Mattie. This is happy birthday to both of you. I know D's is on the 30th so the card should be (!) too early, but I have no record of M's birthday except in early March—I think of you a whole lot, not only on birthdays, and wish you strength and happiness in coming days. I honestly don't think that length of life is important. Very much love from Beatrice." Then she drew the symbolic Beetle, which had been the mark of her childhood.

I spoke with her again on the phone and I recall her starting our last conversation with the words "Fancy hearing from you again." She was already some way off, and next time I rang it was Richard who answered. Beatrice, he said, was deeply sedated, but he thought she would know my voice and answer if I spoke to her. But I refused to disturb her. We had really said good-bye already. She died the next day, a week before my birthday, for which she had sent such wonderful greetings.

At her memorial service in the Dwight Chapel of Yale University there was read a poem she had written, when she knew that her death was not far distant:

Let me be like Bach, creating fugues,
Till suddenly the pen will move no more.

Let all my themes within—of ancient light,
Of origins, and change and human worth—
Let all their melodies still intertwine,
Evolve and merge with ever growing unity,
Ever without fading,
Ever without a final chord . . .
Till suddenly my mind can hear no more.

That prayer, to whomsoever it was addressed, was surely answered.

Dear Daddy and Mattie,

This is

HAPPY BIRTHDAY

to both of you. I know D's is on the 30th, so the card should be (!) too early, but I have no record of M's birthday except early march. And I don't have dramatic episodes to recall as D did for me! Anyway, I think of you a whole lot, not only on Birthdays, and wish you strength and happiness in the coming days. I honestly don't think the length of life is important.

Very much love,
from
Beatrice

Last letter written by Beatrice to her father

OBITUARY

Beatrice Muriel Hill Tinsley

Beatrice M. Tinsley, one of the most widely known and respected theorists in modern astronomy, died on 1981 March 23 at the age of 40, following a three-year battle with cancer. Her most untimely passing shocked and saddened all who had known her and had been impressed by the extraordinary energy and verve with which she had pioneered many lines of study in cosmology and the evolution of galaxies.

Beatrice Tinsley was born on 1941 January 27 in Chester, England, the second of three daughters of Edward O. E. Hill and Jean Morton Hill. Her family moved in 1946 to New Zealand and eventually settled in the town of New Plymouth, where her father was an Anglican minister, and later mayor. She received her high-school education in New Plymouth and later attended the University of Canterbury in Christchurch, obtaining her BSc and MSc degrees in physics in 1961 and 1963. From an early age she had shown a special talent in mathematics and an abundance of industry and ambition, and as her interest in mathematics and science developed, so also did her determination to pursue her studies to the highest possible level and to excel and achieve distinction in them. Her exceptional ability and her enthusiastic pursuit of learning led, almost inevitably, to a brilliant scholastic record, and later to an equally outstanding scientific career.

In 1963, having recently married physicist Brian A. Tinsley, Beatrice moved to Dallas, Texas. Finding little opportunity there to pursue her scientific interests, she enrolled in 1964 as one of the first graduate students in the recently established Astronomy Department of the University of Texas in Austin. Despite commuting each week from Dallas and spending only half of the week in Austin, Beatrice mastered the graduate programme with awe-inspiring speed, and in 1967 completed a thesis which was a major scientific achievement, a pioneering study of the evolution of galaxies. Her first interest in astronomy had been in cosmology, but she had quickly realized that further progress in this subject depended on understanding how galaxies evolve, so she devised the technique of synthesizing models of galaxies by putting together the available empirical and theoretical information on the evolution of stars to deduce how galaxies evolve in colour and luminosity. This thesis marked the beginning of modern detailed studies of galactic evolution, and with it Beatrice Tinsley's career in the field was firmly launched. Her thesis contained two major conclusions: (1) the colours of galaxies of all Hubble types can be explained as a result of different histories of star formation without assuming different ages, and (2) galaxies fade rapidly enough that substantial corrections are required when they are used as 'standard candles' in cosmological studies. These conclusions were not immediately appreciated by all, and Beatrice felt at first that it was difficult for her to get her work accepted, but over the next several years her results became well established through further work on her part and confirmation or rediscovery by other investigators.

Family responsibilities brought a brief pause in her career after she adopted a son Alan in 1966 and a daughter Teresa in 1968, but her growing professional ambitions could not be set aside, and within a few years she had resumed her research career with the full force of her prodigious energy, beginning a prolific series of projects and publications that continued until her death. She rapidly established acquaintance with many prominent astronomers, and initiated numerous collaborative efforts combining the expertise of individuals working in diverse areas. All who worked with her were impressed with her broad knowledge and her ability to quickly grasp and synthesize information from many fields. There is not space to even list all the projects on which she worked, but they expanded in many directions the study of galactic evolution and its relations to cosmology. To mention a few examples, several papers studied stellar populations in the solar neighbourhood and in star clusters, in order to obtain improved information about late stages of stellar evolution and the evolutionary history of our Galaxy. An important series of papers on the chemical evolution of galaxies combined concepts of galactic evolution with information on stellar chemical compositions and nucleosynthesis, and provided a careful study of the possible processes and models; these papers emphasized that the simplest models often fail and that realistic models must be more complex, involving features like gas flows and inhomogeneities. Several papers also addressed the evidence concerning the origins of different types of supernovae, and their relation to stellar evolution and nucleosynthesis.

In addition to the effect of luminosity dimming on the use of galaxies as standard candles in cosmology, Beatrice studied the use of the diameters and surface brightnesses of galaxies and the use of galaxy counts and the integrated background light as possible cosmological tests. In all cases similar conclusions were reached, namely that the observations are at least as sensitive to the evolution of galaxies as to the differences between the cosmological models being tested. As a result of this work, it eventually became clear that most 'cosmological' observations actually provide more information about galaxies than about cosmology, and that the evolution of galaxies is actually a very rich subject of study in itself. For example, such 'cosmological' observations as counts of faint galaxies and measurements of the extragalactic background light are sensitive to whether galaxies experience an initial bright flash of star formation or whether star formation occurs more gradually; they are also sensitive to the mix of galaxy types and whether this changes with time. Tentative evidence for an early phase of rapid star formation in at least some galaxies has appeared in some of the data, but the identification of a *bona fide* 'primeval galaxy' undergoing an initial intense burst of star formation, a subject to which Beatrice also gave attention in several papers, has as yet proved elusive. A possible reason for this, discussed in yet another of her papers, is that star formation in young elliptical galaxies occurs not in a single large burst, but less spectacularly in a series of small ones.

Despite her burgeoning career and reputation, Beatrice was never able to obtain academic employment in Dallas, a fact which made her increasingly frustrated, even though she enjoyed a series of visiting appointments at the California Institute of Technology, the University of Maryland, the University of Texas at Austin, and the Lick Observatory. Finally she decided to leave Dallas and seek her fortunes elsewhere, and in 1975 she was appointed Associate Professor of Astronomy at Yale University, an appointment which pleased her greatly and marked the beginning of a very fruitful association with that institution. She interacted with and helped unify the existing activities at Yale in stellar evolution, star formation, and extragalactic astronomy, and contributed much to Yale's eminence in the areas of stellar and galactic evolution. In 1978 she was promoted to Professor of Astronomy, an achievement which finally amply fulfilled her once frustrated ambitions to find suitable academic employment. It was a tragic irony of fate that she learned of her promotion to Professor at the same time that she learned that she had melanoma, a particularly intractable form of cancer that was to lead to her death three years later. Fortunately, her health held out remarkably well for most of that period, and she remained scientifically productive until very near her death in 1981.

Beatrice showed her talents in other ways than her prolific output of scientific papers, of which close to one hundred were published. In 1977 she organized an outstandingly successful conference at Yale on 'The Evolution of Galaxies and Stellar Populations', at which many new trends in extragalactic research were exhibited. Her broad acquaintance with the field and her high standards were manifested in the content of the meeting and the published proceedings which she edited, and which became an important reference in the field. She herself attended a great many meetings as an invited speaker and was well known for her lucid and even inspiring review talks. She served with distinction on university and national committees and became known even in non-scientific circles for her vigour, astuteness, and uncompromising standards. In the Yale Astronomy Department, she served as Director of Graduate Studies, and devoted a generous share of her time and energy to the concerns of the graduate students. Mindful of the help she had received from more senior astronomers earlier in her career, she gave much help and encouragement to students and younger colleagues. She initiated a series of weekly student-faculty lunches, hosted gatherings with visitors, and took students to meetings and introduced them to other astronomers and promoted their work. Young astronomers anywhere in the world might receive a letter from Beatrice commending them for a piece of good work and urging them to continue their efforts; she did not regard them as rivals but rather as co-investigators in the greater enterprise of understanding the Universe.

Perhaps one of her greatest contributions to science does not even appear in print, being alluded to only in the many acknowledgments at the end of papers where her name is mentioned. A great many people were stimulated and inspired by her vitality, her joy in the pursuit of knowledge, and the enthusiasm that she transmitted to others. All avenues of study were to be pursued with vigour, and many projects were launched or strongly influenced as a result of her initiatives. She provided the focus and, directly or indirectly, the driving force behind most of the work on galactic evolution that was done during her lifetime. Moreover, all those who worked in the field knew that their work would receive her close and critical attention, and her comments were often sought and sometimes feared, because she did not tolerate what she considered to be incorrect or inadequate arguments. Although her career was not long in years, it was long enough for her to have a greater impact on astronomy than most astronomers could hope to have over a much longer career.

As remarkable as the rest of her life was the way that Beatrice coped with her final catastrophic illness. As a person of strong ambition, she was initially devastated at the discovery of cancer, but quickly became determined to make the best possible use of whatever time remained. She underwent a series of operations, but her still abundant energy and drive helped her to recover quickly from them, and she soon reappeared in her office ready to carry on with all her normal activities. During this period she produced some of her most significant scientific contributions, including an extensive and widely quoted review on the evolution of the stars and gas in galaxies, the culmination of a long effort to model the stellar content of elliptical galaxies on the basis of detailed spectra, a study of the evolution of disc galaxies and the origin of S0 galaxies, a demonstration of evidence for different proportions of dark mass in galaxies of different Hubble type, and a number of other important works.

In 1980 September her health finally failed when it was found that her cancer had spread to vital organs, and in November a brain tumour left her partially paralyzed and confined thereafter to the university infirmary. Although it had been expected that the subsequent course of her illness would be quick, she instead showed a remarkable improvement and surprised her doctors by how well and how long she held up. She was able to resume some of her scientific activities, such as reading, correspondence, and consulting with students and colleagues. Even the loss of use of her right hand could not stop her, and her final paper, a detailed mathematical treatment of chemical evolution conceived and completed while she was confined to the infirmary, was laboriously written out with her left hand. She died shortly after this paper was submitted for publication.

During her months in the infirmary, it became abundantly clear that she had gained vast numbers of friends and admirers throughout the scientific world, and mail, flowers, and visitors flowed into her room in a steady stream. All who visited her or spoke with her by telephone, even the doctors and nurses, were amazed at her cheerfulness and determination in a situation where she was expected to live only a matter of weeks. Inevitably she suffered moments of depression when her condition took a turn for the worse, but she always bounced right back. She greatly appreciated the attention and support she received from her many friends, insisting that it was the only thing that made it possible for her to appear courageous and cheerful. For her the pain of having to depart from the world at the height of her career was eased just a little by the realization that she was doing so in the full glow of attention and recognition, rather than as a forgotten relic of a past era.

RICHARD B. LARSON
LINDA L. STRYKER

Reprinted from the Quarterly Journal of the Royal Astronomical Society, Vol. 23, 1982, pp. 162–165.

ACKNOWLEDGMENTS

The publication of *My Daughter Beatrice* is a special project of the American Physical Society (APS) Committee on the Status of Women in Physics (CSWP), which works for the education and full participation of women in physics.

The book is a memoir of astronomer Beatrice Tinsley that began as a personal initiative of Mr. Edward Hill, Dr. Tinsley's father. Mr. Hill circulated photocopies of his typescript to a few of Dr. Tinsley's friends in astronomy and astrophysics in 1984. They in turn passed copies to their friends. Soon it was widely appreciated among astronomers, their families, and friends as an extraordinary record of a loving young woman's growth into an outstanding scientist, mentor, and teacher. The CSWP recommended that APS publish the book as part of their program to encourage young people, particularly women, to choose careers in physics and to help their families and teachers understand the preparation, struggles, and enormous satisfaction involved in such a choice.

The APS is grateful to Mr. Hill for allowing them to publish his work, and also to Sandra Faber, Richard Larson, and Lynda Stryker for their contributions. We would also like to express our appreciation to Richard Larson for his careful reading of the proofs.

The book was produced by the skilled staff of the APS and Publications Branch II at the American Institute of Physics publication facility in Woodbury, New York. Special thanks are due to Susan Bruno, Darlene Carlin, Jim Donohue, Georgina Guagenti, and Peggy Judd.

Jeff Howitt assisted with marketing, and Cecil Hoge contributed marketing advice for this unusual book.

The American Physical Society is a non-profit scientific society whose purpose is the advancement and diffusion of the knowledge of physics. This purpose is usually accomplished through scientific meetings and the publication of scholarly journals of physics research. The Society comprises 37,000 member physicists, 90% of whom reside in the United States. Since 1970, the Society has undertaken and published reports on a number of major highly technical APS studies of physics problems of great public importance. The most recent are "Radionuclide Release from Severe Accidents at Nuclear Power Plants" (published 1985) and "Directed Energy Weapons" (available soon).

In addition to technical studies, the APS undertakes various projects to improve education and opportunities in physics, increase the participation of minorities and women in physics, and enhance international cooperation in physics communication and research. *My Daughter Beatrice* is the first general interest book to be published by the APS.

Miriam A. Forman
Deputy Executive Secretary
American Physical Society